THE MARIN MOUNTAIN BIKE GUIDE

WHERE TO GO AND WHAT TO KNOW

FOURTH EDITION

BY
ARMOR TODD

WITH SPECIAL THANKS TO
DAN MILLER

Photographs by
Walter Van Voorhees

THANK YOU

To the Golden Gate National Recreation Area,
Mount Tamalpais State Park, Marin Municipal
Water District, Point Reyes National Seashore and
Annadel State Park for creating and maintaining
this paradise for all to use and enjoy.

ISBN 0-9623537-2-8
Fourth Edition 1991
Copyright © 1988, 1989, 1990, 1991
by Armor Todd

A special thanks to Don Strickler, who provided
the computer expertise to bring this book to market.

Table of Contents

Contents

You Win Some... And You Lose Some

Since the third printing of this book, there have been significant changes in trail access in Marin County. Most of these have occurred in the GGNRA (Marin Headlands). Unfortunately, most have involved trail closures. These trails continue to be listed in the book, though with 'CLOSED!!' stamped across the top of the pages. Maybe we will get them re-opened some day! There is some good news! Two trails have been added in the Headlands: Old Springs (page 21) and a section of Miwok that connects Coyote Ridge with Tennessee Valley (page26). Both are great additions to riding in the GGNRA. A notable change on MMWD lands concerns a favorite trail, Lake Lagunitas (page 52). As of now, two short sections at either end of the dam have been closed to bikes, effectively limiting access to this great entry level ride. You now need to deal with a fairly steep, but short climb across the creek at the north end of the parking lot. We hope to get the original sections re-opened. It is still a beautiful ride and worth the extra effort.

You will notice some new trails in this edition. on the west slope of Mt. Tam and in Point Reyes. Lone Tree (page 31) is a great descent to Hwy. 1 from near Pantoll. McCurdy, Randall, Shafter Bridge and Jewell are all shutes off of Bolinas Ridge and are listed with that trail on page 60. Olema Valley, Stewart, Bear Valley, Coastal and Estero/Drakes Head , on pages 61-65, are all in the Point Reyes National Seashore. All of these trails have always been there, and now you know where they are. Check them out!

General Information

Marin County is unique in that almost the entire western half of the county is undeveloped land that is open to the public. Nowhere else in the world is such an incredibly diverse resource located so close to a major population center. Indeed, on many of the rides described in this book, you will look down on the populous eastern half of Marin and on the office towers of San Francisco, only a few miles away.

The open lands of Marin are basically divided into four segments that are administered by three different agencies. To the south and west are the Golden Gate National Recreation Area (GGNRA) and the Point Reyes National Seashore (PRNS), both in the national park system. In the center is Mount Tamalpais State Park (MTSP), operated by the state. On the north and east are the watershed lands of the Marin Municipal Water District (MMWD). Together these lands form a vast, contiguous area that is laced with miles of fire roads and trails that are perfect for mountain biking.

This book provides basic information about these trails and fire roads: distances, surface conditions, degrees of difficulty and access points. These are by no means all of the ridable trails in the southern Marin area. We must keep some secrets! They do represent a good cross section of areas and challenges and will provide many hours of great riding. Some recommended loops are described on pages 66-76. You can create your own loops by combining trails on consecutive pages. All the rides are rated according to degree of challenge. **Trail conditions are always changing. Long, hot summers produce hard, scrabbly surface conditions that hamper traction. Mid-winter rains generate deep mud and rushing streams that create new and interesting challenges, and hazards. Trails may become impassable due to landslides, fallen trees or flooding. The author assumes no responsibility for their safety. It is important to be flexible whenever you venture outdoors. Be prepared as you would on any wilderness trip, because that is where you are going - to the wilderness next door.**

All the trails and fire roads listed are open to bikes as of the date of printing, except those marked 'closed'. The situation is under constant review and revision. The author cannot be held responsible for legalities arising from such revisions. Check with local authorities if you have any questions. Let's all ride sensibly and we can add to, rather than lose, the mountain bike trails of Marin.

The Bicycle Trails Council of Marin

Recognizing the need for all users of Marin's open lands to coexist in harmony, the Bicycle Trails Council of Marin was formed. It is a growing community of concerned and responsible cyclists dedicated to promoting safe and sensible bicycle use of these areas. We strongly urge you to join this very worthwhile organization.

The Council at Work for You

A couple of years ago, in response to the rising cresendo of user complaints, the MMWD decided to close the Old Railroad Grade. Disaster! Not only is the Grade one of the most popular routes on the mountain, it is also the access point to almost everywhere else. The fledging Trails Council struck a deal with the MMWD and quickly organized a series of informational barricades to educate and control riders. 'Manning the barricades' became a weekly duty for many of us. We spoke to all user groups, signed up new members and conducted detailed usage studies. The crisis was averted. Since then the Council has been quietly lobbying behind the scenes to challenge numerous other threatened trail closures. Speaking as a representative of a large and growing user group, the council has demonstrated that there is power in numbers. The threat is by no means over. The closure of the two sections of trail at the Lagunitas Dam are evidence of that. All it takes is one dumb yahoo careening down the trail and scattering a group of hikers or equestrians and years of painstaking negotiation are negated. Please be conscious of this situation when you ride on the mountain. Don't blow it for everyone else. We can all enjoy this great resource together.

The Bicycle Trails Council of Marin

PO Box 13842
San Rafael, Ca. 94913-3842
or call

456-7512

JOIN NOW!

Things You Will Need...

Helmet

Absolutely wear a helmet! There is no excuse not to. Riding on or offroad involves a risk. Don't risk your head. There are lots of light-weight, cool, comfortable helmets on the market. Buy one and wear it!

Clothing

Layering is the key. The exposed ridges in the GGNRA are frequently cold and windy, while the protected valleys in the MMWD are blister-ingly hot. A day's ride can take you back and forth between the two, so you need to dress for both. Good shorts and a T-shirt are generally adequate for a lot of the year. Winters do require the addition of tights and long sleeves. Polypro- type underwear is always a good idea for cold days. A good windbreaker is the single most important piece of clothing you can carry. It can handle the early morning chill, then stow easily in the afternoon heat. You should always have one when riding in Marin. It will be invaluable on Coyote Ridge in August or anywhere in January. Riding shoes or stiff-soled hiking boots work well on the mountain. Remember that you may, on occasion, be pushing your bike, so hiking boots may be a good idea! Always wear quality eye protection. Prolonged squinting will give you a headache and an errant pebble, bug or branch will do much worse than that. Bicycle gloves are essential. They cushion the bumps and provide protection should you hit the deck. Better shredded gloves than shredded palms. In the winter, full-fingered gloves are a good idea.

Tools

The simple axiom is "if you carry them you won't need them - if you don't carry them you definitely will". Remember that on these trails you will be at least somewhat on your own and out of touch with civilization. That's why you are out here, right? You should keep your bike in good operating condition at all times. There is an argument that good maintenance at home means fewer tools to carry on the road. You be the judge. A good basic kit will include a chain tool, small crescent wrench, allen wrenches (4,5,6mm), slot and phillips screwdrivers, a patch kit, tire irons and an extra tube. You might add a spoke wrench and a couple of spokes. All this will fit nicely into a compact underseat pack. There are now on the market several neat little tools that combine most or all of the above into one handy tool. Check your bike shop. Don't forget the pump! We do not recommend the CO_2 cartridges for everyday rides as they are a one shot deal that become more trash for the environment. A couple feet of duct tape wrapped around the pump is a good idea for badly cut tires, cracked water bottles or brain surgery. Oh, and it is a good idea to have some idea about how all of these work. Bike shops generally offer basic maintenance classes for little or no cost. Sign up for one.

First Aid

A small first aid kit such as those sold in outdoor stores should be sufficient. 'Road rash' , sprains and minor cuts are the most common injuries. An assortment of bandages, gauze, tape, disinfectant, and perhaps an ace bandage will generally be enough to get you back to civilization. Also carry sunscreen and lip protection as you will be out in the elements. A basic first aid class is always a good idea.

Food

Whether you are into nuts and berries or cookies and candy bars, you will eat any and everything you can carry. Power-packed energy bars seem to work well on long rides and an apple is always a treat on a hot day. Bananas are good for a couple of hours in a fanny pack. Dried fruit is always good. Don't try to diet on a ride. You need to eat when you are exercising.

Water

It's simple - carry plenty and drink a lot. You should take a drink at least every fifteen minutes or so, whether you are thirsty or not. Your body needs to replace the water you are losing by sweating. You might try one of the energy replacement supplements that you can add to your water. They seem to help on long rides. We find that it is good to carry two bottles and alternate between plain water and the doctored stuff. Stream water in Marin is definitely suspect, so carry plenty of your own. **Drinking water is available at several points: Rodeo Beach, Muir Beach, Muir Woods, Pantoll, West Point Inn, Mountain Home Inn, Phoenix Lake, Lake Lagunitas, Rifle Camp, Rock Springs, Laurel Dell, East Peak, Five Brooks, Wildcat Camp, Bear Valley and Coast Camp.**

If you are beginning to wonder where you are going to carry all of this stuff, just visit your local bike shop. There you will find an incredible array of packs to fit in every nook and cranny of your bike. We recommend an underseat pack for tools and a fanny pack for everything else. Be prepared.

Rating System

The rating system in this book is by nature subjective and should be followed loosely. All ratings lean toward an optimistic assessment of a rider's ability. Trails are rated from 1 to 6 as follows:

① Beginner - Generally flat terrain and smooth road surface with a few gentle hills.

② Strong Beginner - smooth road surface with longer, slightly steeper hills and longer distance overall.

③ Intermediate - rougher, more technical road surface with steeper, longer hills and faster descents

④ Strong Intermediate - steeper, technical climbing and descents with tight cornering on rougher road conditions; longer distances

⑤ Advanced - Steep, tight, technically demanding trails with loose surface conditions that hinder control; also just some killer uphills and downhills

⑥ Out There - long, very steep climbs and descents on loose, rocky trails with little room for error; remote areas with rugged conditions and little chance for help in an emergency.

The trails are listed in order moving generally from south to north starting at the Golden Gate Bridge and ending near the tip of Point Reyes. You can plan a ride using consecutive pages or use the loop suggestions starting on page 66.

Map Key

Dirt Road	————————————
Paved Road	- - - - - - - - - - - - - - - - -
Parking	**P**
Ranger Station	**R**
Water	**W**

Coastal
FROM CONZELMAN RD. TO BUNKER RD. (FT. CRONKHITE)
1.6 miles

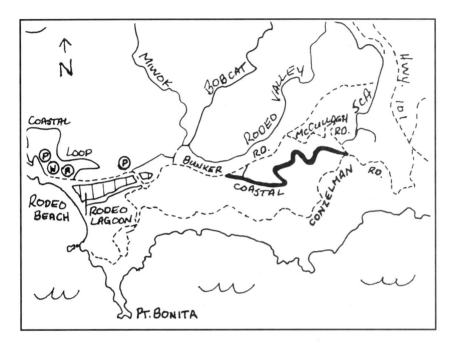

Coastal is a smooth, easy grade with some loose gravel on the turns and great views of Rodeo Valley and the Pacific Ocean. From the parking lot at the north end of the Golden Gate Bridge it is 1.4 miles up to the trailhead (all paved and uphill). The trail starts at the intersection of Conzelman Rd. and McCullogh Rd. and winds down to the old rifle range in Fort Cronkhite. Coming uphill it is the easiest way out of the Rodeo Beach area.

SCA Trail　　　　CLOSED !!
FROM McCullogh Rd. to Spencer Ave.
1.6 miles

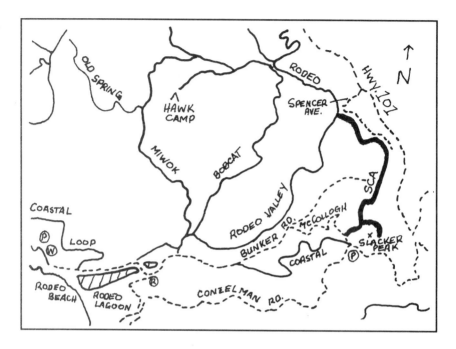

.4 miles - the top of Slacker Peak. This is short and steep- a real grind! The view from the top is worth it though - you are right over the north tower of the Golden Gate Bridge and the entire bay and city are laid out before you.

1.4 miles - the SCA trail from Slacker Peak Rd. to Spencer Ave. The trail starts at .2 miles up Slacker Peak and is a rough fire road narrowing to a tight, steep, scrabbly hill along a narrow ridge with some additional short, steep hills. You are right over the freeway here and have great views of the bay and city. At .75 miles it becomes a genuine single track winding up and down along a steep hillside - great fun!

CLOSED!! **Rodeo Valley**
FROM BOBCAT TO SPENCER AVE.
2.3 MILES

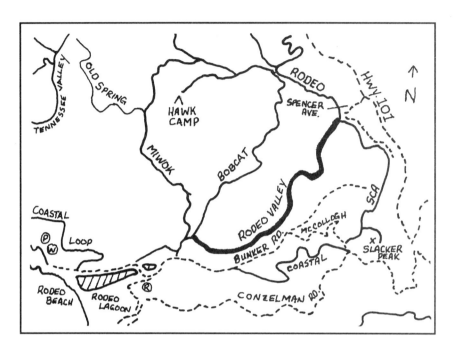

Level and uphill form Bobcat
The first half is flat and beautiful with good traction through a meadow full of wildflowers (seasonal of course). Winter could be a bit muddy. This would be a good first time ride to this point. The second half climbs sharply and the trail narrows, becoming more difficult to ride. At the top you connect with both the SCA and Rodeo and eventually with several other trails on the ridgetops.

Bobcat
FROM TRAILHEAD AT RODEO LAGOON TO TOP
3.4 miles

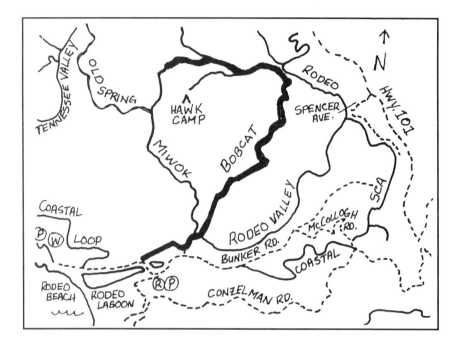

.3 - *branch to Bunker Rd. trailhead*
.5 - *Miwok Trail to left*
.6 - *Rodeo Valley to right*
2.5 - *top of Rodeo Valley to right (no bikes)*
2.7- *Hawk Camp to left (.5 miles)*
3.0- *Marincello to right*

The trailhead is somewhat difficult to see from the road. It starts beside the old warehouses along Bunker Rd. just as the road turns across Rodeo Lagoon. Bobcat is a continuous, moderate uphill punctuated with short, steep sections. Toward the top there are some technical hill sections with loose surface conditions. The road is comfortably wide with great views back down the Gerbode Valley toward the ocean. From the top there are sweeping views of the entire bay area. The top connects with Marincello, Miwok and Rodeo, providing several loop possibilities. Coming down requires care, as the road has some tight, rutted curves on the steep hillsides.

Miwok
From Trailhead at Rodeo Lagoon to Old Spring
1.75 miles

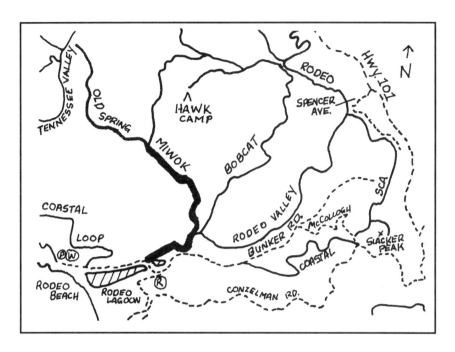

The trailhead is somewhat difficult to see from the road. Please refer to 'Bobcat' on the previous page for directions. This section of Miwok is a nice, wide road with good traction and of moderate steepness. There are some blind corners and lots of equestrian use, so please ride carefully. The upper connection to Bobcat has been closed, so you now have to ride down Old Spring to make a loop. Check page 68 for details. As you ride on Miwok and gaze down into the Gerbode Valley, just imagine that a planned community of 20,000 people came very close to being built there. I'm sure that you will agree that it is much nicer in its natural state.

Coastal
RODEO BEACH LOOP
2.3 miles

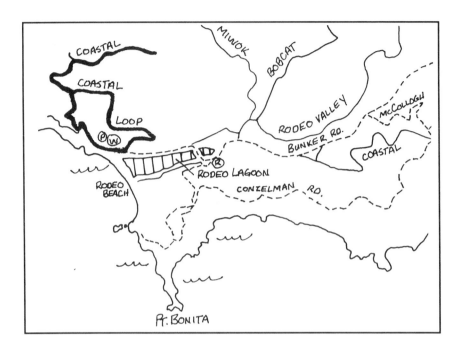

.9 miles - loop continues to the right, the top is to the left
2.4 miles - the top on Wolf Ridge

The loop is a mostly paved, sometimes steep road up from the Rodeo Beach parking lot with some nice ocean overlooks. The road is now open to the top, though you will have to carry your bike over the huge landslide section. Riding to the top is a grind, though the paved descent can be well worth it! There are no loop connections at the top. The lower loop continues behind the old barracks buildings and passes close to the Marine Mammal Center, a worthwhile stop. Here injured seals and sea lionsare nursed back to health to be returned to the wild. After a late afternoon ride, drive across the valley toward the lighthouse for a fabulous spot to watch the sunset.

CLOSED!! Rodeo
FROM SPENCER AVE. TO HWY. 101
1.6 miles

❷

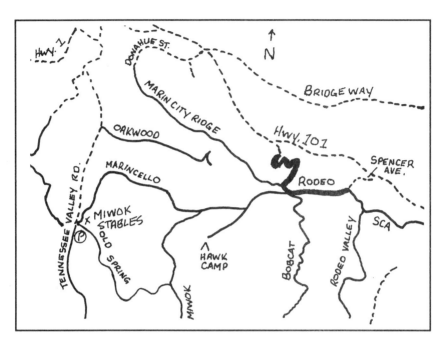

.7 - Bobcat to left
.8 - Marin City Ridge to left

The beginning of Rodeo is a beautiful road through a thick eucalyptus grove high on a ridge. There are gradual ups and downs to the intersection with Bobcat, from where the road drops sharply to the freeway. **There is no outlet for bikes at the bottom!** The best bet would be to turn on Bobcat or Marin City Ridge to continue your ride.

Marin City Ridge
FROM RODEO TO DONAHUE ST.
1.9 miles

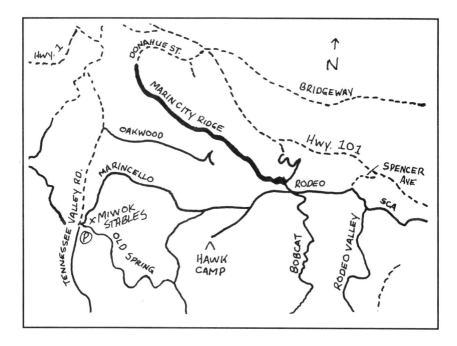

This ridge road winds through eucalyptus groves and offers good traction, easy grades and great views of Sausalito and Tiburon. There is one short, steep spot in the middle. Don't worry if you have to get off and push a little. You can park at the top of Donahue St. in Marin City and have good access to the Headlands area, as the road connects to both Bobcat and Rodeo.

Oakwood (Oak Valley)
FROM TENNESSEE VALLEY RD. TO END
1.6 miles

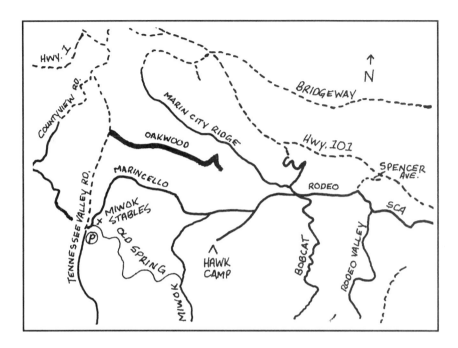

This is a seldom ridden, gradual climb through eucalyptus groves. There is lots of poison oak, but it is easy to avoid, once you know what to look for. This is a good ride to find a secret spot to hang out for a picnic, or a tryst. There is no outlet for bikes at the end, just a rugged hikers only trail up a rough incline studded with railroad ties. Try it for a Sunday morning casual cruise.

Marincello
FROM TENNESSEE VALLEY RD. TO TOP
1.5 miles

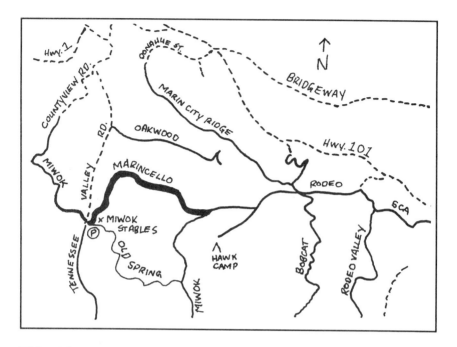

This wide cut in the hillside, once the access road to the planned town of Marincello, is the easiest route up onto the ridgelines from Tennessee Valley. The road starts at the parking lot at the end of Tennessee Valley Rd., off the dirt road to the Miwok Stables. It is a lightly rutted moderate hill with some loose gravel and one short. steep section (sound familiar!). There are great views of Marin, the hills of Napa and Sonoma and the East Bay. Care shoud be taken coming down, as the long straightaways make it easy to pick up speed. The top intersects with Bobcat and opens up a large area for riding. As is the case throughout the headlands, there is equestrian use, so please be courteous and stop if necessary to let them pass.

Old Spring
FROM TENNESSEE VALLEY TO MIWOK
1.2 miles

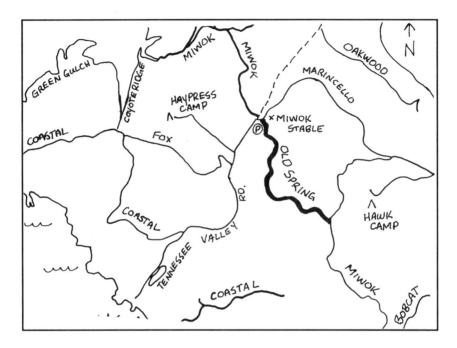

Old Spring is a great little single track up onto the ridge at Miwok. At this time the trail starts right in the Miwok Stables. Look for a path between a hay bin and corral opposite the stable office. There is some talk of relocating the trailhead. If so, it will be close by and well marked. Please respect the horses and BE COURTEOUS! The initial ascent is the toughest part, as the deeply rutted single track climbs from the stable. From here is a breeze for awhile. The trail winds in and out of single and double track with great views down Tennessee Valley and out to the ocean. After a couple more steep pitches you will come to the trail's namesakes, a series of perennial springs. There is always water here. Go for it - they are makeable in any season. You will get muddy! The trail ends at Miwok, from where you can descend into the Gerbode Valley and Rodeo Beach.

Tennessee Valley Trail
FROM THE TRAILHEAD TO THE BEACH
1.9 miles

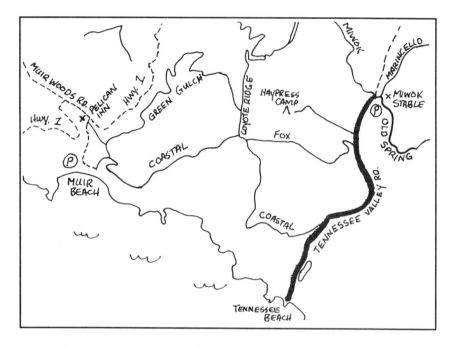

.3 - road to Haypress Camp (,5)
.4 - Fox to Coyote Ridge
.9 - Coastal to Coyote Ridge

Tennessee Valley is a great beginners' trail, except for one hill out toward the beach. This hill looms even larger on the return trip. I still recommend it, especially in the late afternoon, when the valley is particularly beautiful. The first third is paved, then it is smoothly packed dirt with good traction. The trail gets lots of use, so please be courteous. There is a bike rack at the beach, so you can lock your bike and wander for awhile. If you are just starting out, plan to get a bit of a challenge on that hill and thoroughly enjoy the rest. Haypress Camp is a primitive campground in a beautiful eucalyptus grove, less than a mile from the parking lot. It is totally secluded and definitely recommended.

Coastal
FROM TENNESSEE VALLEY TO COYOTE RIDGE
1.5 miles

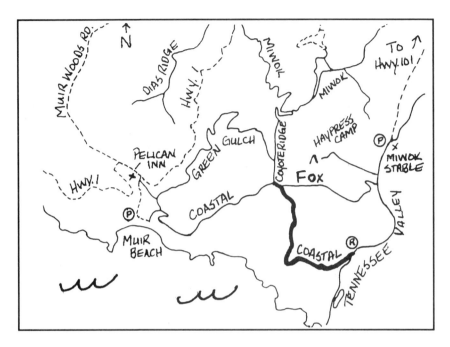

1.4 - right is the top of Fox
1.5 - Coyote Ridge Gate

The beginning of this section of Coastal is a steep, relentless uphill that is loose, gravelly and rutted - remember we do this for fun! The top half is rolling, but generally uphill to the Coyote Ridge gate. Coming down requires being very alert - as the surface is very rough and rutted. There is some equestrian use, so please be courteous. There are fabulous views of the coastline from the top of the first ascent. Take a breather and enjoy the panorama. Also keep a sharp eye out for wildlife. Wildcats are fairly common in this area. Remember that the wind can be howling on the ridges, so pack a windbreaker.

Fox   CLOSED!!

1.1 miles

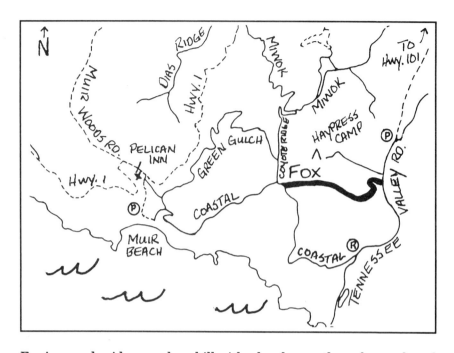

Fox is a good, wide open downhill with a hard, smooth surface and good visibility. It is very easy to pick up a lot of speed, so please ride in control and be courteous to others. The bottom of the trail can get deeply rutted following winter rains, and can become a real hazard. Ride with care. Going uphill is a real grind, though it is shorter than Coastal onto Coyote Ridge.

Coyote Ridge
FROM COASTAL TO MIWOK
2.4 miles

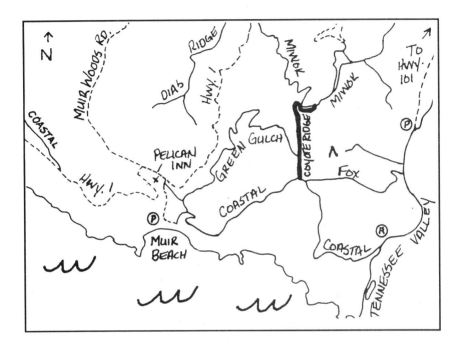

Coyote Ridge is a gradual uphill along a windswept ridge that is among the highest points in the headlands. Stunning views stretch away in all directions. The road surface is smooth and flat with good traction to the top. You will frequently be joined by a herd of black angus cattle along the way and may catch a glimpse of a bobcat. They seem to be fiarly common on the ridge. Beyond the summit the road drops sharply to the intersection with Miwok. When I say 'windswept', I mean it. During the summer the fog and howling winds up here are amazing, and cold. It is great fun to ride in the swirling fog, but you must dress warmly as there is no cover until you get back down.

Miwok
FROM SHORELINE HWY. TO COUNTYVIEW/TENNESSEE VALLEY
3.2 miles

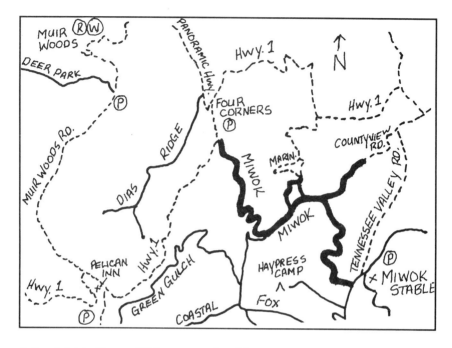

1.5 - right is Coyote Ridge up to the ridge
2.3 - Marin Drive
2.5 - left is to Countyview / right is to Tennessee Valley

This section of Miwok is a good, smooth gradual climb to the intersection with Coyote Ridge, where it drops, sometimes steeply, to Marin Drive. From there it climbs again through the eucalyptus grove to the fork. To the left is the road down to Countyview Drive. To the right is the great little single track that drops down to Tennessee Valley. This section is highly recommended! Tight switchbacks and steep drops end right at the Tennessee Valley parking lot. This whole area is a beautiful corner of the GGNRA, with rock outcroppings, meadows and thick eucalyptus groves. It is an ideal spot for picnicking or just sitting on a rock contemplating...

Coastal
FROM MUIR BEACH TO COYOTE RIDGE
1.75 miles

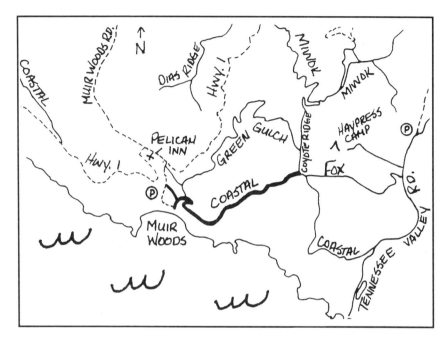

This section of Coastal is extremely steep coming up from the beach. We are talking the Zen of biking here! Put it in low and grind away. And after the initial climb - you climb some more. Going downhill would be quite thrilling, provided you didn't lose control on the rutted surface and hurtle off into the ocean - a long way down! Ride in control. The trailhead is at the south end of the Muir Beach parking lot. You cross the foot bridge, then head up and up, and up. And remember, we do this for fun.

Green Gulch   CLOSED!!
FROM MUIR BEACH TO COYOTE RIDGE
2.4 miles

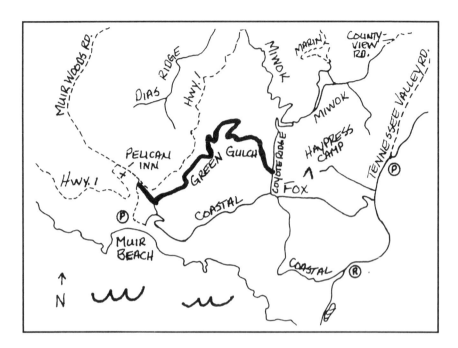

1.0 - take the sharp right turn off the paved road, then the left fork up through the broken pavement.

The Green Gulch Trail starts opposite the Pelican Inn and heads right into the fields of the Green Gulch Farm. Follow the road up through the Zen Center buildings and continue on the pavement as if you were leaving by way of the normal road. Then take the turn described above. There is a trail sign at the turn - though it is a bit hidden in the brush. From this point you are going up - steeply. You will pass Hope Cottage, a spectacular aerie with views forever. It is now a retreat for members of the Zen Center. Cattle are grazed along the trail, a fact that is obvious even when they are not around. Luckily the constant wind keeps the flies away. This is an easier way onto Coyote Ridge from Muir Beach than Coastal. Why not put the two together for a grinder of a loop and have a really big day?!

Dias Ridge
FROM PANORAMIC HWY. TO END
1.9 miles

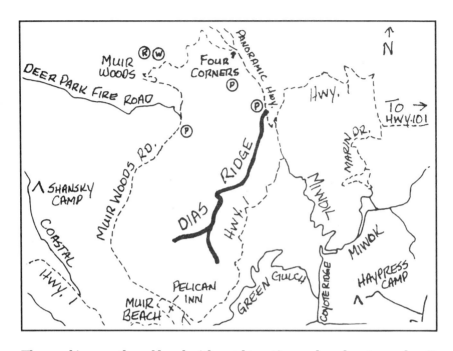

The road is smooth and hard with good traction and moderate grades. It rolls up and down out to the end on a point overlooking Muir Beach and the Pacific. There is no outlet down to the beach. You ride back the way you rode in. There is a lot of equestrian use here, so please ride in control and be courteous. The end of the trail would be a great spot for a secluded picnic.

Coastal
FROM PANTOLL TO HWY. 1 AND MUIR BEACH
3.2 miles

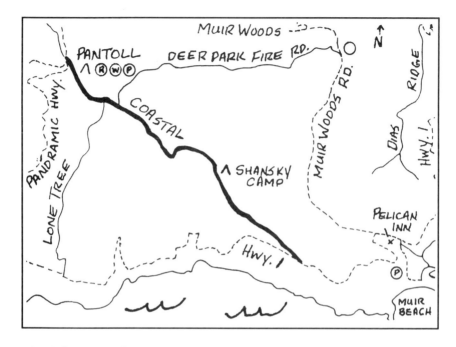

.4 - right turn is Lone Tree
.6 - left turn is Deer Park Fire Road
1.7 - Shansky Camp
2.6 - gate at tilled field, okay to go on

This stretch of Coastal is a long downhill with sweeping curves that can be deceptive. Watch your speed! I have seen more crashes along here than anywhere else, hitting the dirt hard once myself. The turns are off camber and rutted with some surprise dips. Enjoy but be careful. The trail starts at the Pantoll Ranger Station on Panoramic Hwy., where there is ample parking ($5), water and a campground. You head out the paved road through the park maintenance yard, then into a thick stand of pine. Soon you break out onto the grassy ridges of the headlands. The views here are unsurpassed, as the entire ride overlooks the Pacific. Once you get down to Muir Beach, you have a long grind to get out no matter which route you take. Be sure to allow enough time and energy.

Lone Tree
FROM COASTAL TO HWY. 1
1.8 miles

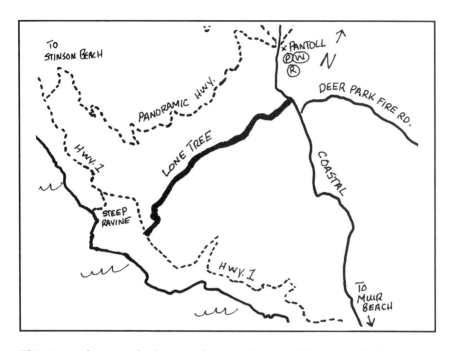

This is an elevator shaft going down to Hwy. 1. The top rolls for a short while and then the bottom drops out and it's 'hold on'! The views alone are worth the ride. You are on an open hillside high above the Pacific with panoramic views from Pacifica to Point Reyes. Of course in the summer the views might not extend past your handlebars, when the fog rolls in. The trail hits Hwy. 1just south of Steep Ravine and about two miles south of Stinson Beach. We recommend riding to either Stinson or Muir and meeting a friend with a car!

Deer Park Fire Road
FROM COASTAL TO MUIR WOODS RD.
2.4 miles

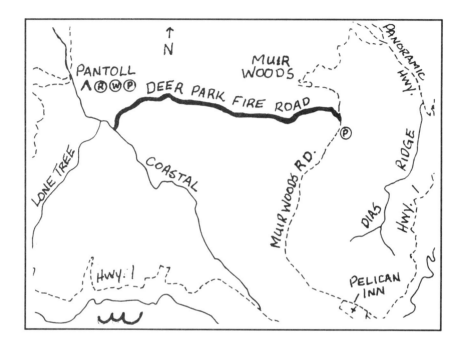

The Deer Park Fire Road is one of my favorite rides on the mountain. The top of the trail winds through a thick and mysterious redwood grove, your passage cushioned with redwood shavings. In the middle you break out onto open hillsides with lots of secluded spots to rest and absorb the beauty. The road is smooth and hard packed with excellent traction. The Dipsea Trail parallels this route, so runners are frequently seen huffing and puffing up to Cardiac Hill. At the bottom you are just a short ride from the wonders of Muir Woods (no bikes - but worth the walk). Going up Deer Park can be a grind, but the scenery is well worth it.

Old Stage Road
1.9 miles

1

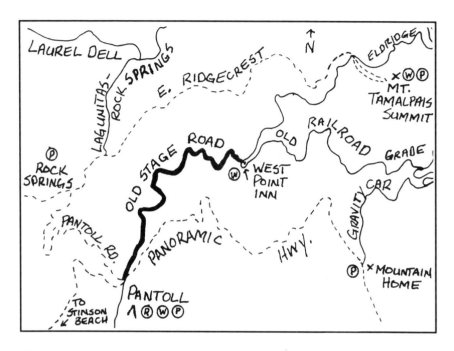

.5 - paved road down to ranger's residence

Old Stage Road, once the route of stagecoaches running passengers down to Bolinas from the West Point Inn, is a gradual uphill from Pantoll. The road is wide and fairly smooth, with good traction. Excellent views extend south to the city. At the end is the West Point Inn, a rambling old lodge from the railroad days. Please see a further description of the Inn on the following page. This would be a great trip for a beginner, with a great destination at the end. At the Inn you connect with the Old Railroad Grade, on which you can continue to the top of the mountain or descend into Mill Valley.

ᴜld Railroad Grade
FROM THE TRAILHEAD TO THE TOP OF MT. TAM
7.1 miles

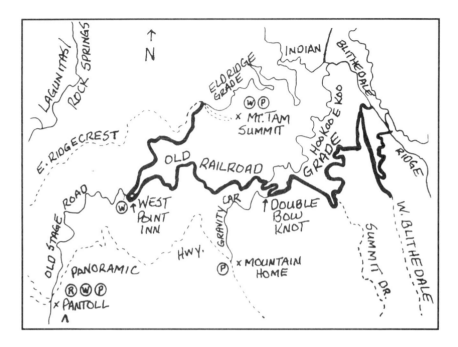

.2 - fork to the right is called 'Tanks' and climbs up to Blithedale Ridge in .7 miles. It is steep and loose (4) and is a quick way over the ridge to the lakes area.

.7 - fork to the right is similar to the former one: .25 miles to Blithedale Ridge and rated 4.

1.9 - pavement stretch: down in Summit to Mill Valley, up is Fern Canyon. We go up.

2.5 - back on dirt road

2.9 - Double Bow Knot: straight is Gravity Car Grade to Mountain Home and Panoramic Hwy. Keep going up to right. The concrete siding here is a good rest stop. It was formerly the stop from which train passengers boarded gravity cars for the ride down into Muir Woods.

3.3 - right is Hoo Koo E Koo

5.3 - The West Point Inn. Stop and refresh. Have a lemonade and granola bar from the kitchen (small donation) and enjoy one of the best views in the bay area. You can even spend the night with advance reservations - ask inside. Closed Monday.

Old Railroad Grade
FROM THE TRAILHEAD TO THE TOP OF MT. TAM
7.1 miles

7.1 - the top at E. Ridgecrest. Turn right and ride the last .25 miles to East Peak, then lock your bike and hike up to Gardiner Lookout - you are on top of the world!

The Old Railroad Grade is the most popular bike route on the mountain. Once the route of the Mt. Tam Scenic Railway, it is a gradual, but continuous climb that is suitable for all skill levels, provided the riders have a bit of stamina. There are several spots to rest and take in the great views as you climb to the summit. At one point, just below the West Point Inn, there is a small spring-fed waterfall that is perfect for a cooling splash on the head. Drinking the water is not advised. The grade is the main route up from the Mill Valley side of the mountain, connecting with many other trails on the way. From Hoo Koo E Koo you can head over to the Marin lakes and central ridges. From Old Stage you can ride out onto the headlands and from the top you can descend to almost anywhere. The West Point Inn is a must stop on the ride. The rambling structure was built as a station for the Mt. Tamalpais Railway, from which passengers could disembark for the hike to the Mountain Theater or board the stage for Bolinas. It is now run by The West Point Inn Association, a volunteer group that dispenses coffee, tea, hot chocolate, and granola bars for a small donation. Leave your change in the can to help preserve this great spot. During the summer and fall they host pancake breakfasts one Sunday a month. The dining area has some great photographs of the train and is a welcome warm spot on a cold day. The covered veranda is perfect for sipping lemonade, enjoying the view and plotting the rest of the ride. Other services include restrooms, water and telephone. Overnight stays can be arranged by reservation. Check with the staff. Weekends find lots of folks stopping here, so there is always someone interesting to talk to and all those cool bikes to look at. (Closed Monday).

Since the Railroad Grade is so popular it sees lots of activity from all user groups. For awhile in 1988 we almost lost it for bicycle use. Please ride in control and be courteous. Watch your downhill speed.

Gravity Car Grade
FROM MOUNTAIN HOME TO RAILROAD GRADE
.9 miles

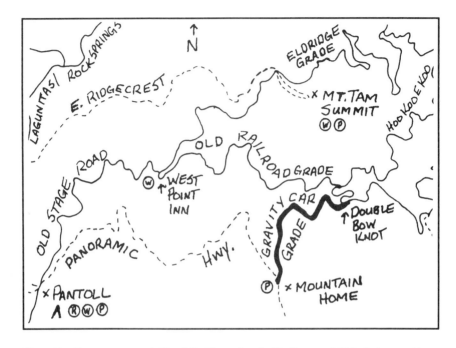

Gravity Cars once met the Mt. Tamalpais Railway at this intersection, called Double Bow Knot, and carried passengers down to Muir Woods. The grade is now a good entry onto the mountain from about halfway up.The road is smooth and wide and climbs gradually to the Railroad Grade. It splits just before getting there and is a bit confusing, though both forks end at the same place. This would be a good way for a strong beginner to enjoy the upper half of the mountain without having to pedal from the bottom. Try riding up to West Point, then back down the same way, or come down Panoramic Hwy. There is parking at Mountain Home. Bikes are not allowed on Gravity Car below Mountain Home.

Hoo Koo E Koo
FROM RAILROAD GRADE TO BLITHEDALE RIDGE
1.9 miles

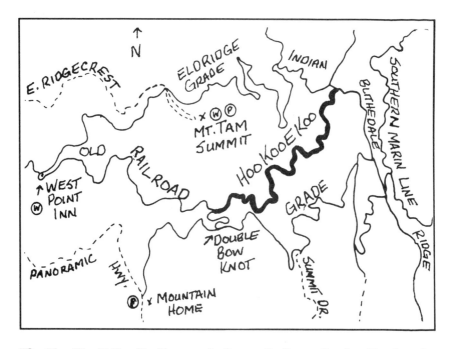

The Hoo Koo E Koo Trail, named after an Indian tribe that lived at the base of the mountain, is a good traverse route to get back and forth between the south and north sides of Mt. Tam. The trail itself is fairly narrow and rocky, requiring alert and skillful riding. There are some short, steep spots, especially near Blithedale Ridge. Once at this ridge, you have access to the whole Marin lakes area, though the ride up Indian is a killer (description follows). Or you can head out onto Corte Madera Ridge and Southern Marin Line. From the Railroad Grade side you can ride up to West Point and head out onto the headlands - a long and wonderful day.

Blithedale Ridge
FROM INDAIN FIRE TRAIL TO END
2.3 miles

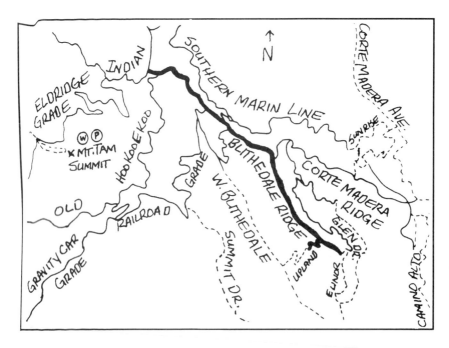

Blithedale Ridge, known locally as Roller Coaster, is just that, a steeply rolling road along the spine of a lower ridge of Mt. Tam. The trail is deeply rutted, loose and scrabbly in parts, especially on the steep parts. This is technical riding. A good loop workout can be enjoyed by riding up Railroad to Hoo Koo E Koo to Blithedale Ridge to Upland Dr., then back into downtown Mill Valley. These ridge roads are tough!

Corte Madera Ridge
TWO SPURS FROM BLITHEDALE RIDGE TO END
.9 miles/1.7 miles

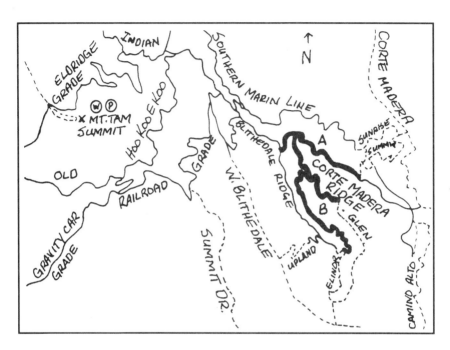

A. Blithedale Ridge to Summit Drive: .9 miles
This spur is a good extension of 'roller coaster' with short, steep ups and downs and some deeply rutted spots. The surface is hard packed for good traction. The trail ends at the top of Summit in Corte Madera, runs down the pavement for a short distance, then continues down to the top of Camino Alto Dr. (an additional .8 miles of steep riding).

B. From the first spur down to Mill Valley by the golf course: 1.7 miles
This is a moderate grade with a smooth, flat surface that runs through a beautiful redwood grove near the bottom. There are some short, steep spots, but you can make it! The right fork is the one to ride - it is longer, with some great ups and downs and you get the redwoods. Access from the bottom in via some very steep paved roads. Use the ridges to come down, not go up.

Southern Marin Line Road
FROM CROWN RD. TO SUNRISE
2.88 miles

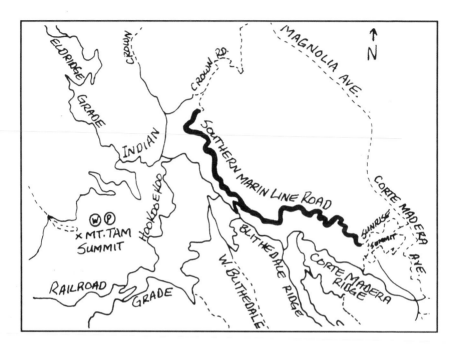

Southern Marin Line would be the perfect road for beginners - if you could ride up to it easily. Unfortunately it is a steep grind up city streets to either end and there is limited parking. Once you get there the road is smooth, hard packed, shaded and almost completely flat - no hills! There are some good views down Baltimore Canyon. Halfway through the trail there is a short, fairly steep spur that climbs to Blithedale Ridge (,25 miles), which then opens up the whole top and south face of Mt. Tam. You might try to find a parking spot near the trailhead and discover the sport of mountain biking - the easy way!

Indian Fire Trail
FROM ELDRIDGE GRADE TO CROWN RD.
1.4 miles

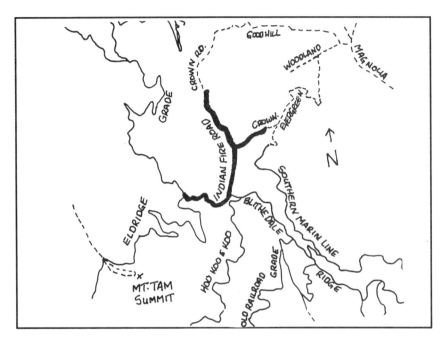

.5 - right turn is Blithedale Ridge down to Hoo Koo E Koo
.9 - right turn drops down to 'other' Crown Rd. (see map).

Indian Fire Road is another of the challenging lower ridge routes on the mountain. The upper half of the road, from Blithedale Ridge up, is very steep and technical. It levels a bit through a small redwood grove, but it is basically an uphill grind to Eldridge. This upper grind is part of the traverse route between the south and north sides of Mt. Tam (Railroad-Hoo Koo E Koo-Blithedale Ridge-Indian-Eldridge). The lower half of Indian is an excellent roller coaster ride along the ridgetop down to Crown Rd. in Kentfield - great fun going down (ride in control).

Eldridge Grade
FROM SHAVER GRADE TO THE TOP OF MT. TAM
5.7 miles

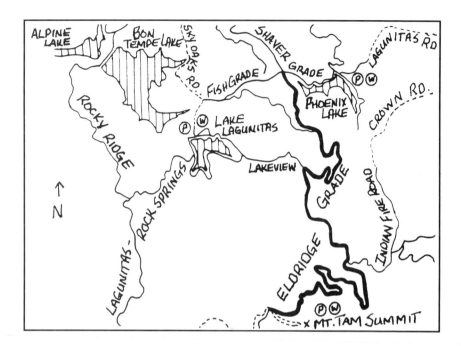

.8 - right turn goes up to Lake Lagunitas via a moderate climb that connects with Fish Grade and Sky Oaks Rd. near the lake. 1.7 miles (2)
2.1 - right turn is Lakeview which descends to Lake Lagunitas. There is one short. steep hill in the middle. You could park at the lake and use Lakeview to access Eldridge to ride to the top of Mt. Tam. .8 miles (3).
*3.2- left turn is Indian Fire Road down to Blithedale Ridge. From here up it is **Uphill Traffic Only** on Eldridge. You cannot ride down from the top.*

Eldridge is a great road up the mountain. It is definitely steeper and more technical than Railroad Grade and reaches the topacross the street from this easier route. The bottom has one little 'whoop-de-doo' from a past landslide- a fun technical challenge. The middle of the route is just a continuous uphill pull with lots of rough, fairly steep and bumpy sections. One climb beside an old water trough will have you puffing! Remember that the road from the intersection with Indian on up is open to uphill traffic only - look for the sign. Once you ascend from there you are committed to descend via another route. The last half mile at the top

Eldridge Grade
FROM SHAVER GRADE TO THE TOP OF MT. TAM
5.7 miles

is very rugged and bumpy - requiring considerable concentration just when you have about had enough for awhile. But now you are on top of the mountain and can chose any number of ways to come down (not, however, on Eldridge). Be sure and ride the last quarter mile on the pavement to the view point and savor your victory! You might even want to hike to the very, very top at Gardiner Lookout and be on top of the world.

Lagunitas/Rock Springs
FROM EAST RIDGECREST DR. TO LAKE LAGUNITAS
3.2 miles

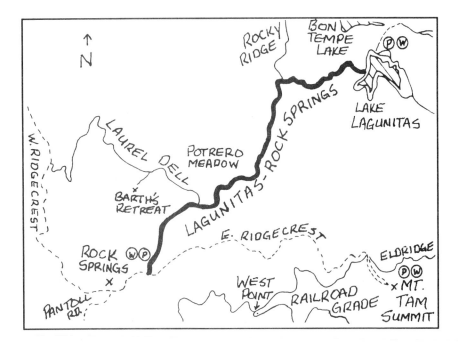

.8 - left turn is Laurel Dell
2.4 - left turn is Rocky Ridge

Lagunitas/Rock Springs is a great. long, bumpy downhill from almost the top of Mt. Tam. Near the top is Potrero Meadow, one of the most beautiful spots on the mountain. The road drops rather precipitously from the meadow, and the surface is washboard rough. Please watch your speed and ride in control. The trail is popular with hikers and equestrians. Riding up is locally referred to as 'taking the elevator to the top' - it is steep, steep, steep. But you do get up in a hurry if you make it. Ride it back down after taking Eldridge to the top - a great day on the mountain.

Laurel Dell

FROM LAGUNITAS/ROCK SPRINGS TO RIDGECREST

2.2 miles

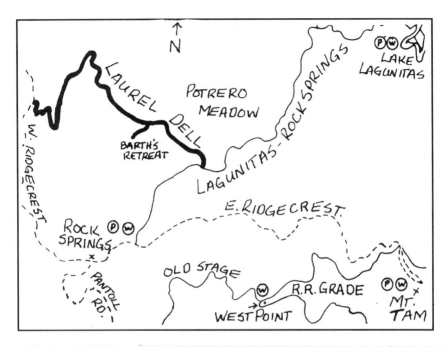

.5 - *left turn in to Barth's Retreat*
1.6 - *Laurel Dell picnic ground*

Laurel Dell is a great intermediate road with a smooth, flat surface and several challenging ups and downs. The road starts in Potrero Meadow and winds through the trees up to a ridge with views all the way to Tomales Bay and beyond. Then it's a great roller coaster downhill to the Dell itself (picnic tables/pit toilets). The west end climbs, at times a bit steeply, to the the pavement at W. Ridgecrest, where you have an incredible view of the Pacific. During the rainy season the creek crossing at the Dell is quite interesting! Check out the loop idea on page 69.

Rocky Ridge
FROM LAGUNITAS/ROCK SPRINGS TO BON TEMPE LAKE
1.9 miles

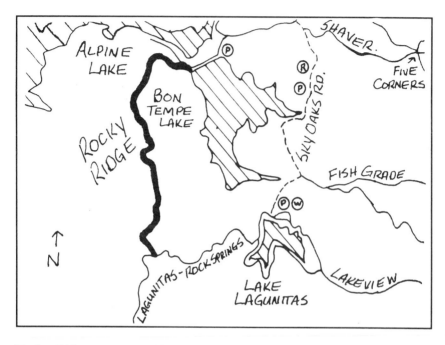

Rocky Ridge is a mix of level, rocky road and very steep, loose, rutted rocky road. The lower half is a real grind up from the west end of Bon Tempe Dam. After spring grading the hill is almost unmakeable, with a deep crushed rock surface on the steep climb. Riding downhill is equally thrilling, what with the front wheel continually sinking into the soft stuff. Winter runoff carves deep ruts into this hill, making it even more of a technical challenge. Above the initial climb the road levels, though the surface is always rocky and loose - hence the name. The ridge is covered with serpentine rock, so it is relatively barren. It gets really hot on those shadeless summer days. Plan on a grind of a great ride.

Shaver Grade
FROM PHOENIX LAKE TO SKY OAKS RD.
2.4 miles

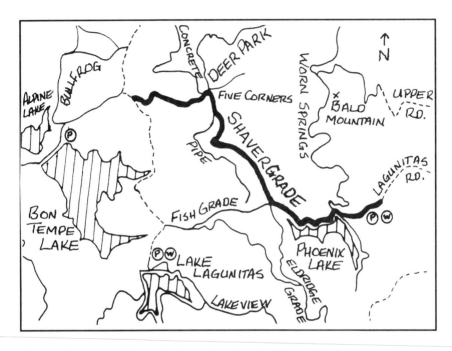

.1 - right turn is Worn Springs Road to Bald Mountain
.7 - sharp left is Eldridge Grade, next left is Fish grade
1.7 - Five Corners

Shaver Grade is probably the most traveled road on the mountain. It is heavily used by hikers, runners, equestrians and rangers with radar guns. A weekend can bring a real crowd here. Weekdays are a pleasure. The trail is a beautiful path through the hardwood forest around the lakes. It winds gradually uphill from Phoenix Lake to Five Corners where it meets several other roads. Uphill from Five Corners it steepens a bit, though the road surface remains flat and smooth. A '2' might be optimistic, but a strong beginner should make it up to the upper lakes. A ride up Shaver to Lake Lagunitas, out Lakeview to Eldridge and then down to Phoenix Lake would be a great ride for a spirited beginner.

Worn Springs Road
FROM SHAVER GRADE TO BALD MOUNTAIN
2.9 miles

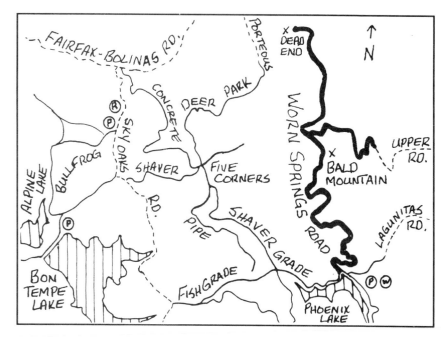

1.6 - left is Worn Springs; right is to the summit
1.7 - the summit of Bald Mountain
1.8 - right turn to Upper Road (to San Anselmo)
2.9 - dead end, no through access

Worn Springs is a long, very steep, exposed uphill grind. We climb it because it is there - also because there is a great view from the top. Be careful on a hot day, as you will be cooking. Rarely will see another person up there. Currently there is no way out for bikes at the north end of the road. There is talk of opening a section down to Fairfax, which would be great. Stay tuned. For now, you either go down via Upper Rd. into San Anselmo or retrace your climb and enjoy the freefall back down. Please watch your speed and ride in control.

Fish Grade
FROM SHAVER GRADE TO SKY OAKS RD.
.8 miles

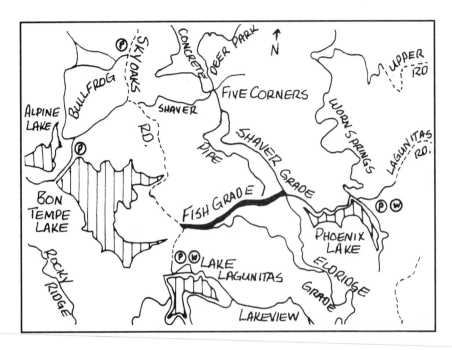

Fish Grade is short and steep, That's it. It climbs immediately from Shaver Grade and keeps climbing all the way to Sky Oaks Rd., a short distance from Lake Lagunitas. It is the shortest way up from Phoenix to Lagunitas. We are talking steep here. Going up requires your granny gear and a positive mental attitude. Coming down requires reasonably good brake pads, as you can get going. There are also some tight turns and a few ruts. There is a lot of trail use in this area so please watch your speed. The road surface is packed and the entire route is in the shade, so at least you won't bake as you grind to the top.

Concrete Pipe
FROM BOLINAS/FAIRFAX RD. TO END
2.6 miles

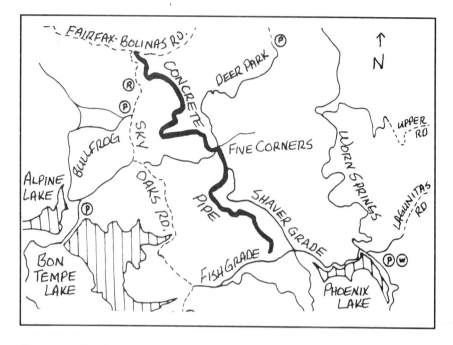

Concrete Pipe is a gentle uphill with a good, flat, smooth surface and no surprises. The road comes through Five Corners and runs together with Shaver a bit before it splits off again to its eventual deadend, close to Fish Grade. There is talk of opening up the last short section so that it will connect with Fish, but not yet. Stay tuned. The last half of the road winds through thick hardwood forest above Phoenix Lake and is quite a nice ride, in spite of the lack of through access. Combinations of Concrete Pipe and Shaver Grade, with their proximity to the lakes, would make perfect riding for beginners and casual riders alike.

Deer Park Road
FROM FROM FAIRFAX TO FIVE CORNERS
1.4 miles

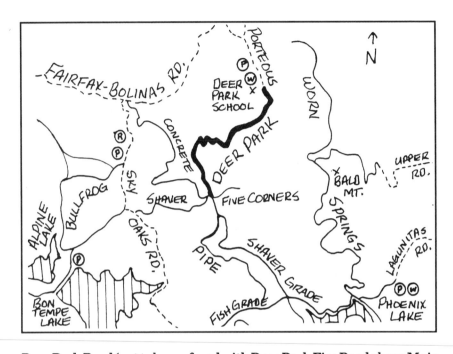

Deer Park Road (not to be confused with Deer Park Fire Road above Muir Woods) is a 'healthy' climb from Fairfax. The road starts at the back of the playground behind Deer Park School at the end of Porteous Rd. Please walk your bike through the school. The road surface is generally smooth and flat, with a couple of lightly rutted turns, and is shaded all the way. The climb might push a beginner, but the extra effort will pay off. This is the best route from Fairfax up to the lakes. There is considerable horse traffic here, so please ride in control and be courteous. From the top at Five Corners you can continue up Shaver to Lake Lagunitas or descend the lower part of Shaver to Phoenix Lake. You could also cruise back out Concrete Pipe to Bolinas Rd. and coast down the pavement back into Fairfax. This whole area is ideal for the 'spirited' beginner.

Lake Lagunitas
AROUND THE LAKE
1.9 miles

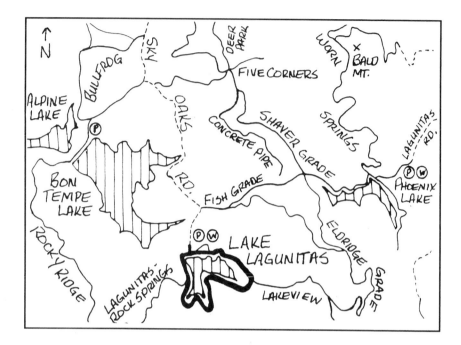

The Lake Lagunitas route is one of the prettiest rides on the mountain. Your initial view of the lake is really breathtaking. It's hard to imagine that the hustle of civilization is minutes away. After parking at the lake ($3.) you head around the lower end of the lot, cross the stream and climb the moderate hill to the lake. This is the only hill on the ride. Now you travel the shores of the lake, gently rising and falling as you go. The road is smooth and hard for easy pedaling. There are three points which involve decisions - splash through the streams or ride the narrow wooden bridges. We find that the streams are much more fun! At the back of the lake the Lakeview Trail heads up to meet Eldridge. Continue to the left. The east shore has numerous spots for a lazy picnic - and great fishing to boot. Please walk your bikes off the road. As you approach the dam again the road narrows, ending in a short staircase. We recommend riding back around the lake and down the hill you rode up. Sweet revenge! The lake attracts lots of folks, so please be courteous to everyone. This is the perfect place to start mountain biking.

Bullfrog
FROM ALPINE LAKE TO SKY OAKS RD.
.9 miles

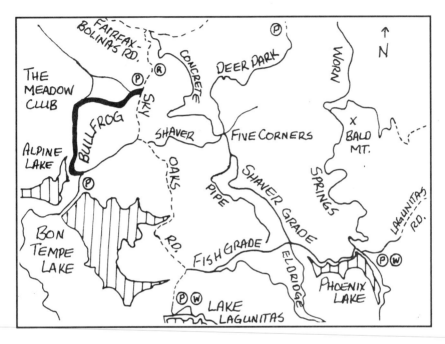

Bullfrog is another of the great beginners' roads that run through the Marin Lakes area. Starting below Bon Tempe Dam at the top of Alpine Lake, it winds gradually up to the Meadow Club golf course, then courses through the low scrub up to Sky Oaks Rd. The grade is always gentle and the road is wide, smooth and level. In the winter there is lots of mud here, so be prepared! Check out the loop suggestions on page 66.

Pine Mountain/San Geronimo Ridge
FROM BOLINAS/FAIRFAX RD.
13.2 miles

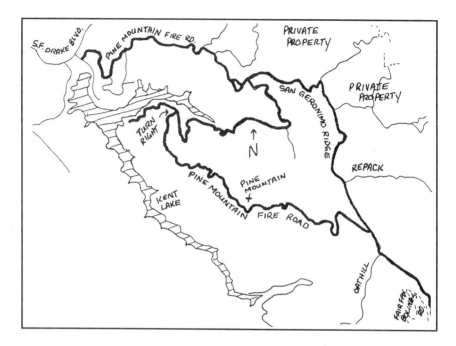

.9 - Oat Hill Road to Alpine Lake
1.5 - turn left at the fork
11.1 - Repack, the quick way down!

Pine Mountain is a long, steep, barren remote and unforgiving trip through some of the most beautiful terrain in Marin. It is partly the remoteness that gives it the tough rating. If you have a problem out here, you are in trouble. Be prepared. The road starts from Bolinas-Fairfax Rd. and heads out San Geronimo Ridge to the fork. The hills are steep! Turn left and keep climbing. You will continue climbing to the summit of Pine Mountain, where you will have sweeping views in all directions. Then it's a great roller coaster along the ridge and the fast drop down to Kent Lake. Turn right at the bottom. The left fork is a dead end. There are three streams to cross before the long, long grind up. At the top of the hill you turn right. Going left or straight will take you down to the dam at Kent Lake via a very tough ride of 3.3 miles, ending at Shafter Bridge near Samuel P. Taylor State Park. We go to the right and continue the loop on the 'fairly' level San Geronimo Ridge. You finish by dropping down a loose, rocky descent to the fork and then retrace your route to the trailhead.

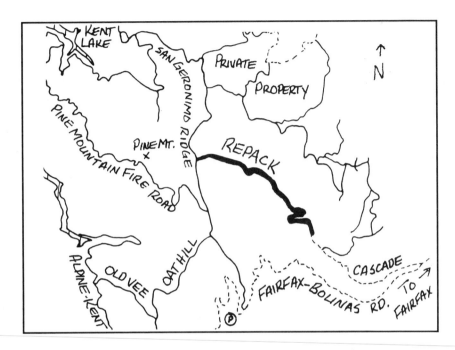

Repack is the legendary downhill made famous by Gary Fisher, who completed the descent in record time in the not too distant past. This is the downhill on the mountain, though current regulations forbid such kamikaze freefalls. The road is extremely steep and twisting, with several off camber, blind turns and a very rough, washboard surface. A lot of the road is covered with thick dust (or winter mud) and loose rock, further hampering traction. Near the bottom you attempt three stream crossings. I say attempt because winter rains could render these very interesting! This is definitely for downhill only. You can certainly ride up, but why? Ride any of a variety of routes up to San Geronimo Ridge, then ride to the top of Repack. You will get plenty of uphill on the trip.

Oat Hill Fire Road
FROM SAN GERONIMO RIDGE TO END
2.9 miles

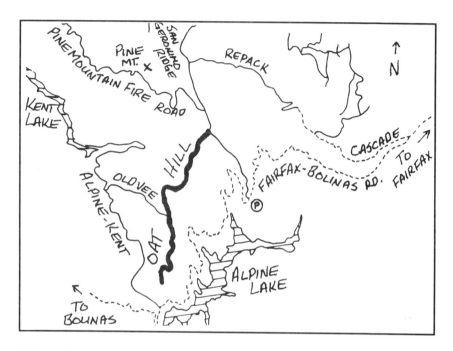

1.7 - right turn is Old Vee

Oat Hill is a good, smooth, wide fire road that wanders up and down a ridge and eventually descends to Alpine Lake, though you can't make it all the way down to the lake without turning off. To get to the start of the road is quite a grind, as you have to climb San Geronimo Ridge, but the views and lack of people are worth it. The road is rolling with well-banked turns and great traction (seasonal). This is a great intermediate ride. At 1.5 miles you pass Old Vee on the right. This is the only way out, unless you backtrack. If you continue straight the road ends in a 'hogback' ridge - a steep, unridable descent that drops to Alpine Lake. Take Old Vee. There is talk of opening a series of trails in this area to bicycle use. They will be a great addition to our ridable terrain. Stay tuned.

Old Vee Fire Road
FROM OAT HILL TO ALPINE-KENT PUMP ROAD
1.3 miles

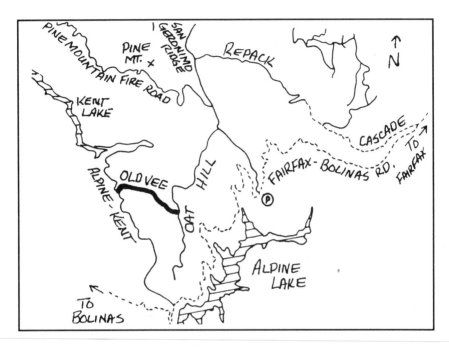

Old Vee is straight down. The road is moderately steep, with a couple of tight hairpins and a loose surface. I is really not all that difficult. You just need to be on your toes, and your brakes! This is the only way down from Oat Hill to Alpine Lake. Riding up Old Vee is makeable, but a real grind. Assuming you start this trip from San Geronimo Ridge, you can ride down Oat Hill, then Old Vee to the Pump Road to Bolinas-Fairfax Rd., then take the pavement back up to the trailhead - also a long grind. This remote corner of Marin is 'real grinds' in all directions!

Alpine-Kent Pump Road
FROM FROM ALPINE DAM TO END
4.5 miles

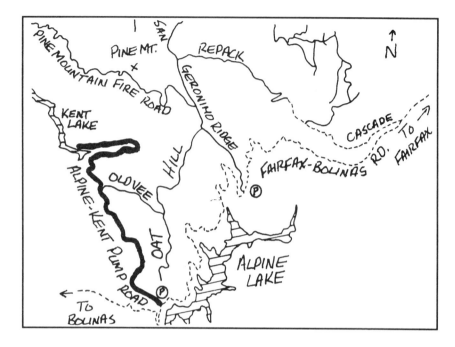

.3 - left goes back to the dam
2.3 - right is Old Vee up to Oat Hill

Alpine-Kent is the one beginner ride out in this section of Marin. It is totally flat for most of the way, with gentle hill at both ends. The road drops a bit from the dam, then levels out as it winds through the thick trees along the creek feeding Kent Lake. Most of the trip is shaded and has the 'feel' of someplace else - like the Sierra. You end with a gradual descent to the lake itself, where the road ends. If you are just starting out, park at the dam and do this ride. It is a great introduction to the sport, as the route is easy and the scenery beautiful. Remember to pack a jacket, as it can get cool in the trees. And bring food and water. There are no services out here. Better yet bring a picnic and hang out at the dam after the ride.

4

Bolinas Ridge
FROM BOLINAS/FAIRFAX RD. TO OLEMA
11.2 miles

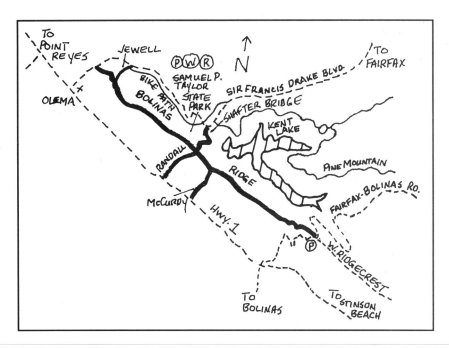

4.5 - *left is McCurdy*
6.5 - *left is Randall*
7.2 - *right is Shafter Bridge*
9.9 - *right is Jewell to Samuel P. Taylor State Park*

Bolinas is the most varied and beautiful ride in the county. It requires some planning or a lot of riding, as it will leave you a long way from where you started. It runs basically downhill from Bolinas-Fairfax Rd. to Olema, though there are some sharp little climbs on the way. You start in towering redwoods, break out onto manzanita covered ridges with forever views, then dive back into some incredible redwood groves, all the while glued to the twists and turns of the well packed road. Riding through the trees gets a bit bumpy, as you bounce aling the root-filled trail. Slow down a bit and learn to pick a smooth line. Slowing down is important here as the ridge is well traveled by hikers and horses alike. Please ride in control. You will soon emerge from the deep shadows of the redwoods out onto the high grass covered ridges, with great, sweeping descents and great views north to Tomales Bay and Bodega Head in the distance. You will have to dismount for a few cattle gates, and even dodge

Bolinas Ridge
FROM BOLINAS/FAIRFAX RD. TO OLEMA
11.2 miles

the cattle themselves on occasion. Remember it is their field - you are the visitor. Please close the gates behind you. You will finish the ride at Sir Francis Drake Blvd. above Olema, where there is parking for about ten cars. Now you can ride back up - for 11.2 miles, or return via Drake or Hwy. 1 and climb back up to the trailhead. Each alternative makes for a long ride. Try parking at the Drake end and doing the uphill first, or park a car at each end and shuttle. Either way the Ridge is worth it. During the ride there are four turnoffs that you will pass. The first is McCurdy, which is a 1.8 mile elevator shaft down to Hwy. 1 at Dogtown. This is a big challenge either up or down with huge erosion gullies and steep hills. Since the ridge is so nice, we wonder why anyone would leave. The next one is Randall, which is a steep 1.6 mile drop to Hwy. 1, but much more rideable and actually very fun. This hits the highway at the millpond made famous by the skinny-dipping sixties, about three miles south of Five Brooks. The third drop is Shafter Bridge, which drops quickly down to Sir Francis Drake Blvd. in 1.7 miles. The road is very steep and twisting, so be in control. It is a good connection to Drake if you need to get a head start back home. You can also connect to the western end of Pine Mountain above the Kent Lake dam, though this is recommended for serious riders only! The last turnoff is the Jewell Trail that is a fairly gentle descent into Samuel P. Taylor State Park. As you descend to the trail, it actually looks as if it is the main road as the Bolinas Ridge Trail does a tight left turn here. Jewell is the way to go in either direction if you start your ride in the park, which is a good idea since there is ample parking ($5.), restrooms, water, camping and picnic grounds. Jewell connects with the Cross Marin Bike Path in the park, which is a great ride in itself. It is perfectly flat and paved and would be a great family ride. You must ride Bolinas Ridge!!

Olema Valley Trail

FROM HWY.1 (DOGTOWN) TO FIVE BROOKS
5.5 miles

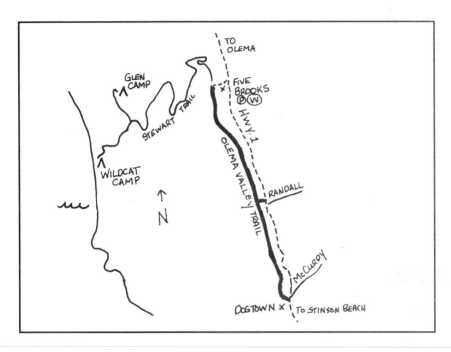

The Olema Valley Trail would have to be pretty tame, Right? It parallels Hwy.1 up the Olema Valley and doesn't really climb or drop anywhere. Wrong! This is a great ride! A genuine single track for most of the way, the trail splits verdant meadows and misty glens, crosses rocky creeks and present enough technical challenges to satisfy anyone. And there is a great downhill at the end. The great part is that anyone with reasonable riding skills will have a good time. We suggest parking at Five Brooks and riding south on the Hwy. 1, then back on the trail. Be alert for the trailhead. It is just beyond a large GGNRA sign at the base of the Dogtown hill about five miles from your start. If you pass the Dogtown Pottery sign, you just missed it. This is not a winter ride, unless you like lots of deep mud. Try it in late spring through the fall. And please respect the 'No Bikes' signs on the various intersecting trails.

Stewart Trail
FROM FIVE BROOKS TO WILDCAT CAMP
6 miles

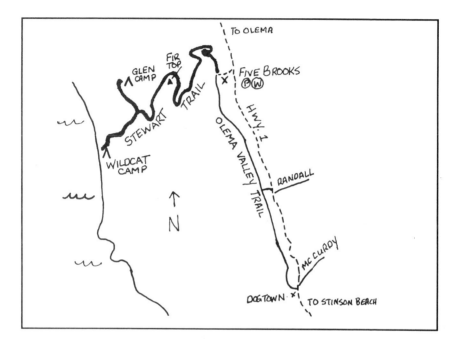

Stewart is a long. gradual climb to the summit of Firtop, 3.8 miles into the ride. The road is wide and smooth. There is horse traffic here, so please be courteous. There is a beautiful meadow at the summit that begs one to take a break. You will definitely take one on the way back! The long descent to the beach is punctuated by some steep pitches. At 5.2 miles you will intersect with the road to Glen Camp, a little over a mile up. It is open to bikes and very pretty, but we came here to go to the beach, right? So stick to Stewart and the reward is just around a couple of corners, and down some more steep drops. The beach at Wildcat Camp is spectacular, and usually deserted. A walk south on the beach will bring you to Alamere Falls, a waterfall onto the beach! You might wonder why such a bucolic place is so deserted. Well now you have to climb out and you will know why! It is up, up, up and more up. This is a wall! But once at the top you get over three miles of great traction, smooth descent to Five Brooks. Please watch your speed. This is prpbably not a summer ride, as the wind and fog will be a bit chilly. Try it in spring and fall.

Bear Valley

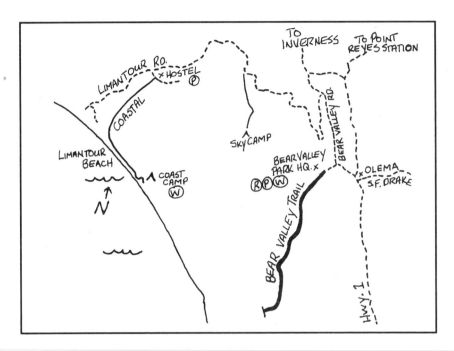

Bear Valley is probably the best ride in the county for the first time rider, or for a casual ride to a great picnic spot. The trail is well packed and smooth, with only a slight rise in the middle at Divide Meadow. And the scenery! You are riding in a veritable jungle of lush greenery, alongside a meandering brook. The meadow is a wonderful spot for a break, or better yet that picnic. Huge expanses of lawn roll up to towering pines. It really is a beautiful place. The gently descending trail hugs the creek as it winds through the sylvan landscape to the ocean. Unfortunately, bikes are not allowed all the way. The trail ends in a clearing where there is a bike rack to lock your steed for the final one mile hike to the beach. Maybe someday... For now we retrace our ride up to the meadow and coast back to the car.

Coastal
FROM LIMANTOUR HOSTEL TO END
3.2 miles

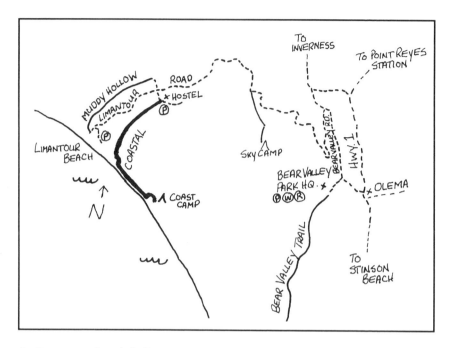

At last, another '1'! Coastal is definitely for the novice rider and for anyone who likes a casual ride ending at the beach. The trail starts opposite the Limantour Hostel. There is limited parking at the hostel and more parking at the Education Center a half mile ahead. Coastal is a wide, smooth easy-pedaling cruise down to and along a berm just above beautiful Limantour Beach. The ride ends at Coast Camp, a cozy campground tucked behind a hill at the beach. The facilities are 'primitive', i.e. pit toilets, BBQ's, water, tables and storage lockers. Even if you don't stay overnight, bring a picnic. You can afford the extra weight on this ride. We highly recommend this ride for beginners, though not perhaps in summer, when the wind and fog would be a bit chilly. Spring and fall are absolutely spectacular.

Estero Trail/Drakes Head
FROM TRAILHEAD TO END
4.5 miles

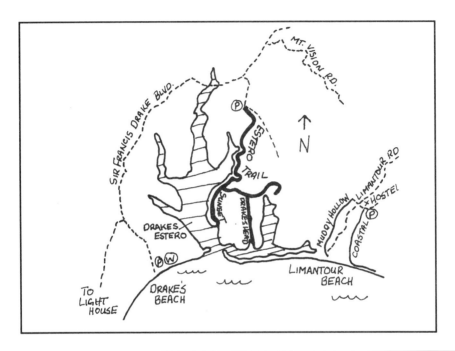

2.3 - Sunset Trail
3.1 - Drakes Head Trail

The Estero Trail takes you out onto the headlands overlooking Drakes Estero and the ocean. It is quite open and dramatic, and very exposed. Take a windbreaker. The road to the trailhead is off S.F. Drake Blvd., just beyond the Mt. Vision turnoff. The trail rises and falls as it weaves its way over ridges and across inlets. There are cattle gates and cattle. Though never too steep, the hills can sneak up on you. The Sunset Trail is an easy descent to a hidden beach, though there is lots of poison oak at the end. The Estero Trail from the Sunset intersection is confusing, as cattle tracks head off everywhere. Watch for 'walk-throughs' in the fences and little blue and white arrows. The Drakes Head Trail kind of peters out just short of the cliffs at the ocean. We suggest hiking the last bit for an incredible view. Don't worry about your bikes. There is nobody out here! Remember that any ride in Point Reyes is subject to extreme wind and cold, so plan accordingly.

Beginner
Marin Lakes Loop
6.1 miles

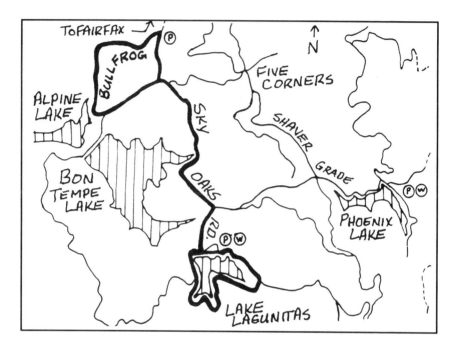

This is a good loop for the first time rider. Park at the Lake Lagunitas parking lot ($3.). Retrace your drive in on Sky Oaks Rd., taking advantage of the paved ride to familiarize yourself with the gears and brakes. Turn left down the dirt road to Bon Tempe Dam. At the bottom of the hill take the right fork and pick up Bullfrog. Pedal up the gentle hill to the Meadow Club, then on to Sky Oaks Rd. Turn right on the road and head back to Lagunitas. Now cross the creek on the bridge below the dam and climb up to the lake. It is a bit steep here, so don't be afraid to walk a bit. Now you get to circle the lake on one of the most beautiful trails anywhere. At the other end we recommend that you retrace your route around the lake so you get to enjoy it one more time before you break out the picnic and relax in the sun.

Beginner
THE WEST POINT LOOP
7.5 miles

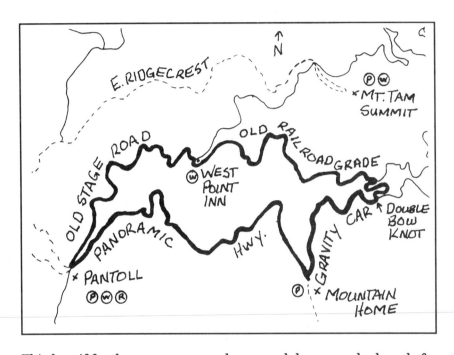

This loop if for those newcomers who can pedal up a gradual grade for awhile - and want to enjoy a fabulous view when they get to the top. Start at the Mountain Home parking lot and head out Gravity Car Grade (it's across the street, uphill from the Inn). At Double Bow Knot pick up the Railroad Grade and head toward West Point. The concrete siding here is a good spot to rest. The West Point Inn is the highest point on the ride. Stop and peruse the great photographs of the train days and sip a cool glass of lemonade on the veranda. What a view! Now pick up Old Stage (down by the picnic tables) and descend to Pantoll. From here the fun begins - the great paved descent back to Mountain Home. Watch out for cars and tight turns. This is not for the first time rider, but anyone with a little road riding experience will appreciate the thrill. Enjoy!

Intermediate
GERBODE VALLEY/TENNESSEE VALLEY
7.8 miles

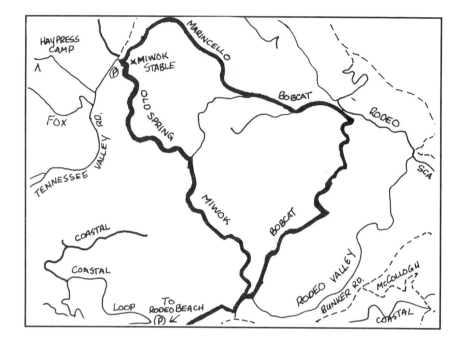

This loop includes a tour of the Gerbode Valley, once the site of a planned city of 20,000 people. You will soon appreciate the fact that it was never built. You can park at Rodeo Beach, then retrace your drive in back to the east end of the lagoon. The trailhead is just beyond the old warehouses on the north side of the street. From here climb up Miwok, noting the bucolic Gerbode Valley below you. A the top you will pick up Old Spring for the highly entertaining, mostly single track descent into Tennessee Valley. The water hazards are makeable! Please be courteous at the stables. Now you get to climb Marincello back up onto the ridge. Check out the views of Marin and the wine country in the distance. The Bobcat descent is a great way to coast back down into Rodeo Beach. Watch your speed and enjoy the ride.

Intermediate

Laurel Dell/Lagunitas-Rock Springs
4.5 miles

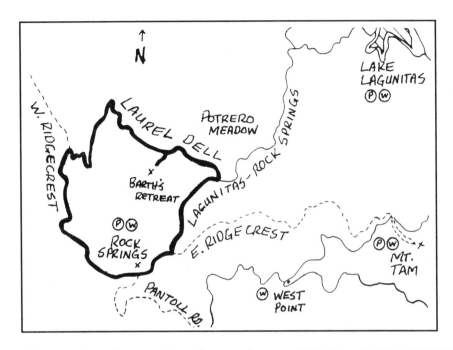

This is a short, but very fun ride near the top of Mt. Tam. Park at Rock Springs and head east on E. Ridgecrest toward the summit of the mountain (East Peak). You will pass the Mountain Theater and soon spot a fire road climbing to your left. Head on up and steel yourself for one more short, steep climb. Now hang on for the fast descent into Potrero Meadow. Catch Laurel Dell to the left, just as you enter the meadow. Get ready to enjoy the great roller coaster ride along this trail. There is a picnic spot in the middle that makes a good rest stop. You will have a stream crossing that, depending on the season, might be very interesting! Then you climb again to W. Ridgecrest and an absolutely breathtaking view of the coast and ocean from the ridge, about 2,000 feet up. Head south on the pavement and you will soon be back at your car. Now drive back out to the ridge and spread out your picnic. Mountain biking is tough!

Intermediate
THE LAKES TOUR
9.9 miles

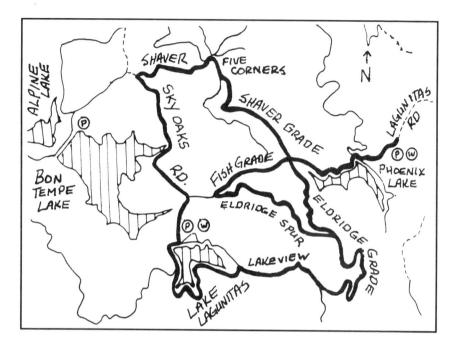

This is a good two hour, late afternoon ride through the beautiful Marin Lakes area. Park at Phoenix Lake and head up Shaver to the top, passing through Five Corners on the way. Turn left on Sky Oaks Rd. and follow the pavement to Lake Lagunitas. Cross the stream below the dam and climb up to the lake. Ride around the lake and turn right on Lakeview, just after the third stream crossing. Head up Lakeview to Eldridge. There is a hill here, but you can make it! Drop down Eldridge to the next intersection and take the left fork up to the top of Fish Grade. Now take the drop back down to Shaver and Phoenix Lake. You could also continue down Eldridge, bypassing the last climb. This alternative includes a great litte technical section at the bottom.

Intermediate
Over the Mountain and Back
15.9 miles

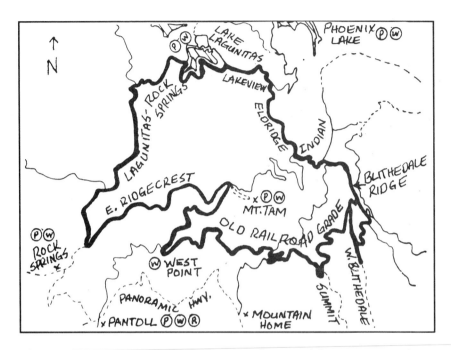

This is a long journey that takes you to the top of the mountain, down again, and halfway up again before dropping back to your starting point. You start at the Railroad Grade in Mill Valley and climb all the way to the top. At E. Ridgecrest Dr. you turn left and ride the pavement to Lagunitas-Rock Springs. This is a bit of a grind. Be alert for the trailhead. It's opposite the large dirt parking lot as you descend. After a short climb to the top you have a three mile descent to Lake Lagunitas. Watch your speed. Turn right and ride around the lake, turning right again on Lakeview. Head up to Eldridge and start climbing again. Take the left fork at Indian and begin your final descent. It gets steep and bumpy here. Catch the right turn onto Blithedale Ridge, pass the first right (Hoo Koo E Koo), then take your choice of the two spurs that drop to the right, back down to Railroad - all in a day's ride!

...ermediate
COYOTE RIDGE LOOP
5.8 miles

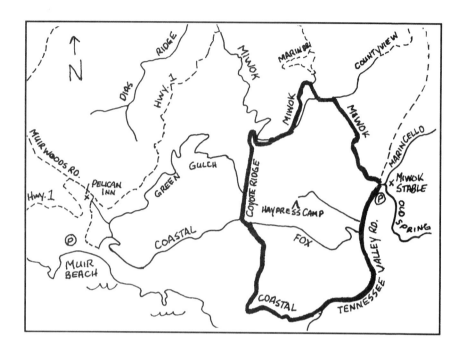

This high intermediate ride starts and ends at the Tennessee Valley parking lot and features some of the best views in the headlands. From the lot, head down the paved road toward the beach. Stay to the right at the fork and head up Coastal, just beyond the ranger's house. This is the climb of the trip and it is a climb! We highly recommend a break at the top of this first climb. The view is a worth a stop. Now follow the road as it climbs more gently up to Coyote Ridge. Head up the ridge (more climbing!), then drop down to Miwok. Follow Miwok through the eucalyptus grove (watch the steep drop!) and head to the right. At the fork, go right and get ready for the great little single track descent that returns you to the parking lot. A great ride!

Advanced
THE NORTH SLOPE PLUS ROCKY RIDGE
16.3 miles

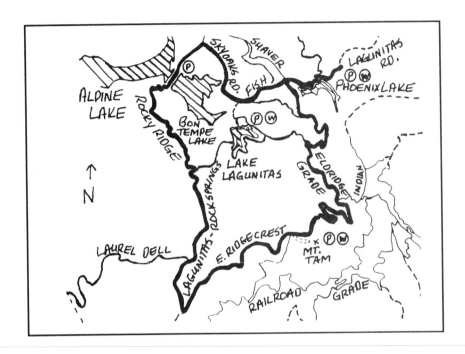

A strong intermediate should be able to handle this tour of the north side of Mt. Tam, though Rocky Ridge is steep and technical. Start at Phoenix Lake and ride up Shaver to Eldridge. Turn left and ride Eldridge to the top of the mountain - no problem! At the top turn right on E. Ridgecrest and ride the pavement to Lagunitas-Rock Springs. The trailhead is opposite the big dirt parking lot as you descend. After the short climb you get a long downhill to Rocky Ridge. Turn left out onto the ridge and bump along the rough trail to the steep, loose, rutted downhill. Ride with care. At the bottom, cross the Bon Tempe Dam and ride up to Sky Oaks Rd. Turn right and follow the pavement to the 'T' intersection at the end. A right turn goes to Lake Lagunitas. Turn left down the pavement and drop down Fish Grade (first left) to Shaver and back to Phoenix Lake.

Advanced
Mt. Tam to Tennessee Valley
20.1 miles

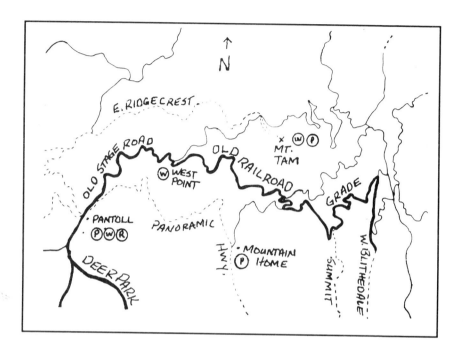

This is a long day with two major climbs, the second being tougher than the first. You will start in the sheltered arroyos of Mt. Tam and end up on the windswept ridges of the GGNRA - one of my favorite itineraries. Start at the Old Railroad Grade and head up to the West Point Inn. Drop down Old Stage to Pantoll, pick up Coastal through the park maintenance yard and break out of the trees onto the ridge. Here you can choose between two great descents - turn left onto Deer Park or go straight onto Coastal. Deer Park is steeper and prettier, with a long, twisting run through the redwoods. It is a great ride, and will leave you on Muir Woods Rd. with a two mile paved shot out to Muir Beach. Coastal is almost as fast, with sweeping turns and incredible views of the Pacific. The road ends at Hwy. 1, where you will turn left for a very fast paved descent into Muir Beach. You will just have to do this ride at least twice to sample both trails! You will do well to rest a bit at the Pelican Inn at the beach (closed Monday) because the big grind is coming. As you are relaxing on the sunny front lawn of the Inn, glance southward and notice an impossibly steep road pasted on the hill at the far end of the beach. Guess

Advanced
Mt. Tam to Tennessee Valley
20.1 miles

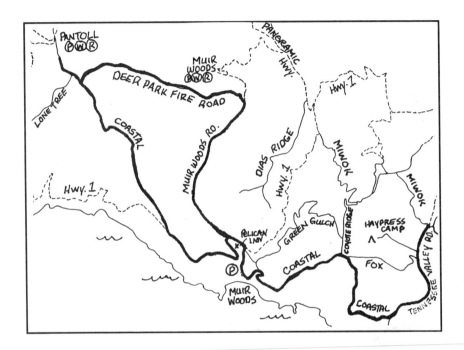

what?! That's Coastal and you get to climb it. Tha trail starts at the south end of the Muir Beach parking lot, across the foot bridge. It is a granny gear grind - the Zen of mountain biking. After considerable pain you will reach what you think is the top. Then you get to climb some more! Winter rains effectively reduce this trail to a waterfall, so plan on a dry day. Eventually you will reach the top at the Coyote Ridge Gate. Keep right and descend Coastal all the way down to Tennessee Valley. You might want to stop on the way for the great views. Once down you can turn right for the quick run out to the beach, or just head up to the trailhead and the paved run back to Mill Valley and your starting point. This has been a day!

Advanced
Pine Mountain Loop
13.2 miles (with options)

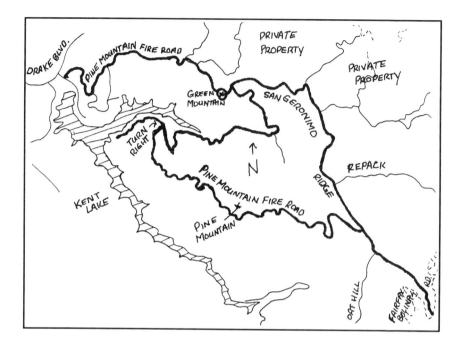

This is the big one. 13.2 miles of loose rocks, steep climbs, technical descents, exposed ridges and vast loneliness. And now we have added some new tortures to this great ride! You are on your own out here. That is the reason for the '6'. The loop starts at the Azalea Hill parking area on Bolinas-Fairfax Rd., about a mile above the Meadow Club, in Fairfax. Ride across the street and begin the climb. You will immediately feel the loose, rocky surface. Get used to it. The road climbs and falls for half a mile or so, then climbs in earnest up a steep, rutted hill. Just beyond the top is the left turn for the Oat Hill Fire Road. Continue straight to the next fork. The trail signs are under the big tree. Take the left turn here and start to climb some more. Feel that loose stuff? After much grinding and perhaps a bit of walking you will be at the summit of Pine Mountain, surrounded by incredible views. Check out the view north to Tomales Bay and Bodega Head. Now you get to enjoy a stretch of great roller coaster ups and downs and turns. Ride in control! The road takes a sharp right and drops quickly down to Kent Lake. Turn right. The left turn is a dead end. The next mile or so winds through the canyon, gradually climbing as you cross three streams. Then comes the big climb out. The road up is wide and smooth, which is good because the grind up is long and hard enough as it is. At the top you will turn right. The options here extend to the left and straight. Both ways meet on the far side of Green Mountain, which is right in front of you as you ponder your choices. By taking either of these you are leaving the loop, but embarking on a great ride through some even less traveled country. The road climbs and drops like a roller coaster and eventually descends to Peters Dam, at the head of Kent Lake. You will ride out to Sir Francis Drake Blvd, just west of the town of Lagunitas and have a long ride home. It is well worth it to check out this area, though it is really for very strong riders only. We turn right onto San Geronimo Ridge and endure a series of 'moderate' climbs as we head back. There are a few turnoffs here heading down to the left (north), though most end in private property and should be avoided. They are technically legal, though they would leave you on the wrong side of the hills and a long way from home. Continue along the ridge road as it curves around to the right and starts dropping back to your starting point. On your left you will pass the top of Repack, that kamikaze descent into Fairfax. If you are in a hurry...! Otherwise continue down the very rugged and rocky road to the original fork and retrace your route to the trailhead. Feeling good? Feeling bad? Are you feeling at all?

The Geology

Mt. Tamalpais was formed more than twenty million years ago by the gradual upheaval of the ancient sea floor caused by the actions of 'plate tectonics' and accompanying volcanic activity. The mountain is not a cohesive mass, but a jumble of solid chunks in a matrix of pulverized rock that is testimony to its violent birth. The primary rocks found on the mountain are: sandstone and shale, formed from the sediments of the ancient sea floor; chert, the shiny, brittle remains of sea animals; serpentine, formed by the combination of water and the mantle rack, peridotite. This bluish, gray-green rock is abundant on the mountain and is particularly noticeable in that, since it makes poor soil, it creates whole hillsides of 'dwarf' vegetation.

The Climate

Characteristic of the Mediterranean region of Europe, the Mt. Tamalpais area is blessed with mild, wet winters and warm, dry summers. The rainy season extends from October into April with rainfall averaging between 42 and 52 inches through the various microclimates. Winter temperatures are balanced through the region with highs in the 40's and 50's. Summer, however, finds widely varying temperatures as the fog and wind blanket the coastal hills and valleys up to the ridgelines while the interior plateaus, shielded by the bulk of the mountain, bake in the seasonal heat. The same day may find the western solpes shivering in the 50's while a few miles away, the lakes area is sweltering in the 90's. This obviously presents an interesting situation for the mountain biker, as many rides will traverse both areas within an hour or two.

The History

The Mt. Tamalpais region was originally settled by the Coastal Miwok Indians, with evidence of habitation going back 7,000 years. No settlements have been found on the mountain itself, suggesting that it may have been considered sacred. The legend of the 'Sleeping Lady' holds that the mountain saved the life of a Miwok girl, thus giving the mountain its oft used nickname.

Sir Francis Drake landed at Drakes Bay on the Marin coast in 1579 and recorded the "thick mists and most stinking fog", though no mention was made of the mountain itself. Like so many days during the summer today, it was most likely hidden by those "stinking fogs". By the mid-nineteenth century, adventurers in the area were regularly hiking the trails of the mountain, though many were "satisfied with the view from

from halfway up". Such was the rugged nature of hiking on Mt. Tam. In 1896 the Mill Valley and Mount Tamalpais Scenic Railway began its famous runs up the mountain. For over thirty years the 'Crookedest Railroad in the World' carried passengers up to the platform at Double Bow Knot, from which they could board the gravity cars for the trip down to Muir Woods. Continuing on to the West Point Inn, adventurous souls could disembark to hike to the Mountain Theater or board the stage for the wild ride down to Bolinas. A spectacular hotel once graced the summit of the mountain at the end of the line. The graded roadbed for the train still remains and has become one of the most popular bike trails on the mountain - The Old Railroad Grade. The concrete platform at Double Bow Knot and the West Point Inn also remain, serving as welcome way stations for weary cyclists.

Mt. Tamalpais State Park (MTSP) was officially created in 1931, largely through the efforts of the Tamalpais Conservation Club and William Kent, a local civic leader and congressman. The park now occupies over 6,000 acres with many miles of fire roads suitable for mountain bikes. When considered in conjunction with the neighboring GGNRA, MMWD and PRNS, the Mt. Tam region is a paradise for mountain bike riding. The park is open from one half hour before sunrise to one half hour after sunset. Parking at the Pantoll Ranger Station is $5. There are campsites in a few locations. Call the park for information at (415) 388-2070. Please obey all regulations when using park lands.

The Marin Municipal Water District (MMWD), chartered in 1912, is now the sole supplier of water to southern Marin County and the administrator of over 60% of the land shown on Mt. Tam maps. Several miles of great fire road riding cover these lands. Five of the districts seven reservoirs are on the immediate north side of the mountain and provide a scenic backdrop for many of the rides described here. The area is open the same hours as MTSP. A $3. fee is collected for cars driven into the lakes area.

The Golden Gate National Recreation Area (GGNRA) was founded in 1972 and encompasses lands on both sides of the Golden Gate. The Marin Headlands area, just north of the bridge, provides miles of fire roads and some single tracks with unsurpassed views of San Francisco and the Pacific. The headlands were primarily developed by the army for coastal defense. Portions of many of the forts are still in use today, though for more peaceful purposes. Thankfully, due to the army's 'occupation', the land remains essentially undeveloped today. Developers have long coveted this wonderful stretch of coastal hills so close to the city. As you ride along either the Bobcat or Miwok Trails in the bucolic Gerbode Valley, consider that for awhile in the mid-60's an entire city for 20,000 people called Marincello was planned for the valley. Marincello Road, described herein and planned as the vehicle access to the town, is evidence of how close this travesty came to being a reality.

Point Reyes National Seashore (PRNS) was established in 1962 and encompasses some of the most wildly beautiful scenery on earth. Once you crest the ridge and drop down into the valleys of the ocean side of the peninsula, you enter a different world, seemingly in a different time. There is an almost primordial feeling hanging with the moss in the trees. Though not well traversed by trails open to mountain bikes, the park is worth a visit and the few trails that are open offer a unique and rewarding adventure.

Muir Woods National Monument (MWNM), founded in 1907, is located in a pocket between the GGNRA and MTSP. It is off limits to bikes, though it is recommended as a stop at some point in your riding. Lock your bike at the gate and stroll through an awe inspiring stand of giant coastal redwoods along crystal clear Redwood Creek. Though often crowded, it is a welcome respite from the windswept ridges of the headlands.

The Flora

The vegetation of Mt. Tam and surrounding areas varies greatly depending on a specific location's orientation to the mountain and the sea. Hillsides of the GGNRA and western Mt. Tam are barren, save for a blanket of annual grasses and windscaped scrub. The strong winds of summer and thin soil on the ridges support little else. Protected valleys in this same area, however, are home to the mighty coastal redwoods, tallest of all trees. Some reach heights in excess of 300 feet. In the cool shade of these lofty sentinels dwell ferns and wildflowers reminiscent of a rain forest.

The plateau areas around the lakes accumulate eroded soil from the hills and support a hardwood forest of oak, bay, buckeye and madrone, trees whose great spreading arms provide welcome shade from the blazing sun. North and east facing slopes are covered with forests of Douglas fir and tanoak, mixed with beautiful manzanita. Bike trails on these slopes are characterized by a deep cushion of pine needles and bark shavings that soften your passage through the trees.

And everywhere there are flowers, far too many varieties to mention here. From hillsides of golden poppies, to shaded glens of wild iris to ubiquitous Indian paintbrush, Mt. Tam is host to a myriad of colors, shapes and sizes that cover the land with color from February through the summer.

And now for the bad news. There exists throughout Marin a plant whose brilliantly red autumn leaves bely a most nasty character - poison oak. It is almost everywhere, preferring the dry shaded hillsides and revines. Do not touch it! Contact with the leaves or stems will cause an ugly, itchy, blistering, weeping, thoroughly disgusting and miserable rash that can take weeks to go away. This is not fun stuff. Although some are immune, don't press your luck. Learn to identify its distinctive three leaf cluster which changes color with the season and steer clear. There are various things to do if you think you have come in contact with some. Try squriting the area off with water from your bottle immediately. Ask your doctor or pharmacist for more information.

Another potentially nasty problem is blackberry. Your riding will eventually lead you to discover a blackberry patch. Good for you, as the hot days of summer plump the berries to succulent perfection. Enjoy, but be careful. The vines are studded with razor sharp thorns and are so tangled as to make one shudder at the thought of falling into one.

The Fauna

Mount Tamalpais and the surrounding ridges and valleys are home to many species of animals. Remember that you are the visitor here, so please do not disturb them.

Brown pelicans, seagulls, cormorants and terns, among others, swoop and dive along the ocean's shore and occasionally stray to the lakes. In the adjacent salt marshes, snowy egrets and the majestic great blue herons silently stalk their prey, accompanied by several types of migratory waterfowl. Overhead in the valleys and along the ridges soar the ever-present turkey vultures, those great, black scavengers. It is quite exciting to round a corner and surprise a flock on the ground. Their ensuing scramble for the skies, right in your face, cranks up the heart rate a bit! Sharing the thermals with the vultures are red-tailed hawks, patiently cruising in search of the careless deer mouse. The headlands is a principle 'flyway' for hawks and other raptors as they pass through the bay area on their annual migrations. There are days when hundreds can be seen in a few hours. Mating pairs of osprey occasion the lakes. After a hard ride you can relax on the shores of Lake Lagunitas and watch as they dive for fat trout. The trees are full of smaller birds; boisterous jays, finches, robins, wrentits and flickers. On late evening rides you will occasionally see barn owls in the eucalyptus groves.

Mule deer are everywhere on the mountain and in the headlands and probably in your backyard. Ranging in color from white to dark brown, they will be your constant companions. Small mammals like raccoons, skunks, opossum, jackrabbits and squirrels also abound. There are bobcats, and if you are lucky you will see one from time to time. They seem casually unafraid of you and will frequently let you come quite close before they bound off into the underbrush. The more rugged and remote corners of the region are reportedly home to a mountain lion or two. Sightings are rare. Maybe you'll get lucky!

Rattlesnakes are not common on the mountain, though they are around. I have seen two in several years of riding. Both were on heavily used sections of trail; one less than fifty yards from the West Point Inn on Old Stage and one on the Lake Lagunitas Loop. Kingsnakes, garter snakes, gopher snakes, striped racers and rubber boas round out the snake population. You will see them mainly in the spring, if at all. Summertime heat brings out hundreds of lizards on the dry trails around the lakes. At times the trail seems to come alive beneath you. Be nice and try to avoid them. Wet winter days will occasionally produce newts on the very wet trails. These strange creatures are almost translucent and are very slow moving as they make their way through the mud. When you ride across the dam at Lake Lagunitas or Bon Tempe check out the turtles basking in the sun on the logs. And when riding by the streambeds, listen to the deep croak of the bullfrogs.

There are several nature and wildlife guides available that go into much greater detail about the flora and fauna of Mt. Tam and environs. Most are fanny pack size and will enhance your enjoyment of our wilderness areas. A pair of compact binoculars is also a good addition to your gear.

About The Author

Armor Todd, a resident of Mill Valley, has lived in Marin County for eleven years. A lifelong cyclist, he first discovered the backroads of this area via road bike in the early eighties. After a few tours of Ring Mountain on the ten speed, the first mountain came home in 1984. The road bike has only just been updated and sees very limited use.

A member of the Bicycle Trails Council of Marin, IMBA and the Rails to Trails Conservancy, Armor is a concerned advocate of keeping Mt. Tam and all areas open to mountain bikes through responsible riding, trail maintenance and open communication with all user and management groups.

With his partner, Dan Miller, Armor operates Wheel Escapes, a mountain bike rental and touring company in Larkspur. They offer premium rentals for on and offroad and specialize in packaging custom tours for corporate and social groups in Marin, the wine country, Lake Tahoe, or wherever a group wants to go. For more information you can contact Wheel Escapes at (800) 582-2453.

Phones and Phone Numbers
EMERGENCY: 911
all are (415)
GGNRA Fort Cronkhite (Marin Headlands): 331-1540
MMWD Ranger Station: 459-5267
MTSP Pantoll Ranger Station: 388-2070
PRNS Bear Valley Headquarters: 663-1092
Samuel P. Taylor State Park: 488-9897

Public Telephones:
Fort Cronkhite (Marin Headlands)
Mountain Home
West Point Inn
East Peak (Mt. Tam summit)
Muir Woods
Muir Beach
Phoenix Lake
Lake Lagunitas
Pantoll
Bear Valley
Five Brooks

The

MARIN

MOUNTAIN BIKE GUIDE

Annadel State Park

NORTH BURMA TRAIL
1.63 miles

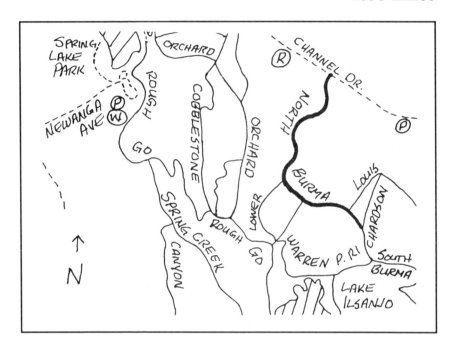

Start at Channel Drive
.71 - North end of Live Oak Trail ❶
1.2 miles - south end of the Live Oak Loop ❷
1.53 miles - Lower Steve's S Trail ❷
1.63 miles - Warren P. Richardson Trail ❷

Bottom is very technical and fairly steep and strewn with large rocks. This is very bumpy riding. There is one waterfall section that is unrideable for all but expert riders - don't be disappointed to walk it - all of us did! The bottom is in the shade - so at least you are not baking while you are grinding. The section between the ends of Live Oak is less steep and is easier to ride though still rocky - so you have to pay attention to hold the narrow line through the bumps. Section on to Steve's S is wide and fairly smooth with good views down to Lake. This is easy cruising, but remember to watch for the rocks. Single track through the trees to the left is just short trail that cuts the corner to Steve's and is smooth, easy and short. The last tenth of a mile is a short sweet shot with the usual rocky surface.

LIVE OAK TRAIL
1.1 miles

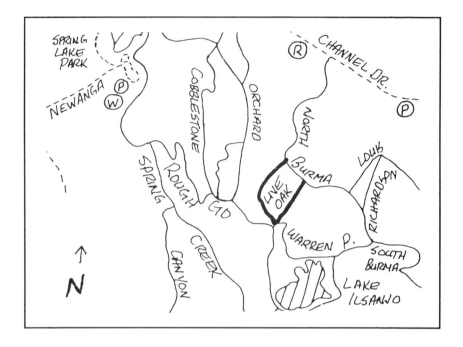

Start at north end at N. Burma
.72 miles - Warren P. Richardson Trail ❸
1.1 miles - south end at N. Burma ❶

Live Oak starts as a single track through trees, then breaks out onto the edge of False Lake Meadow as a double "wagon track". There are great views as you traverse the meadow, but watch out, as you soon drop into tight rut. It is an interesting sensation as you ride along this tight track through a 'semi tunnel' of reeds that are about five feet high. During mid-winter this is no longer a 'False Lake'. It is mostly under water! Pay attention to gearing as you then climb a sharp uphill with limited traction through the grass. The top half of the trail, from Warren P. Richardson back to N. Burma, is a wide flat and smooth fire road through scattered oaks with views of Lake Ilsanjo - easy pedaling. The view from the top is great, looking west toward Sebastopol and the coast.

COBBLESTONE
1.8 miles

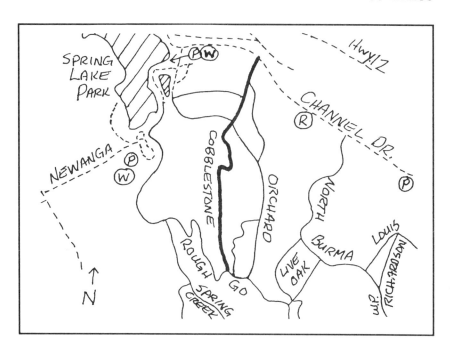

From Channel Drive to Rough Go
.8 - Orchard Trail   ❹
1.8 - Rough Go   ❺

Cobblestone is an extremely rough, rocky mostly single track uphill that will probably require some walking. The trail levels out a bit toward the top, becoming more of a fire road. It is still bumpy and technical. This would be an interesting downhill - good practice for your trials skills. Ride with care! Just after you start up the trail there is a single track that heads out to the left. This simply parallels the marked trail, meeting Orchard up the hill. Take either one - they are both a grind!

ORCHARD
1.4 miles

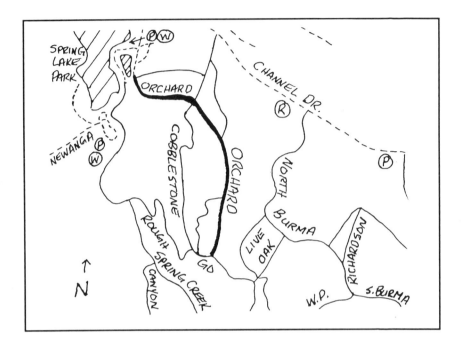

Cobblestone to Rough Go   ❺

Orchard, like its neighbor Cobblestone, is essentially unrideable in its lower reaches. The single track lower portion is solid rocks and very little trail - maybe possible for an expert, but not for us! Toward the top the surface improves considerably, widening to become a reasonably smooth fire road. This would be a great downhill for most of those with intermediate and above skills. This kind of low speed, technical downhill riding is great fun, and good for politics. You get to challenge yourself with a tough test, and you present no threat to other users because of the slow speeds involved. We encourage you to think of downhill riding in these terms - slow and skilled rather that fast and loose. From the lower end of Orchard, at Cobblestone, a road actually continues northeast across Cobblestone and a meadow toward a small hill. This extension is an easy run to the top of Violetti Rd., just uphill from the entrance to Spring Lake Park. This is an another way up into Annadel, though it is not recommended for beginners. About two thirds of the way up Orchard from Cobblestone you will see a single track heading off to the right. This is a great ride that winds through the trees and rocks and ends at Rough Go, very near to the end of Orchard itself - take it!

STEVE'S TRAIL
.21 miles

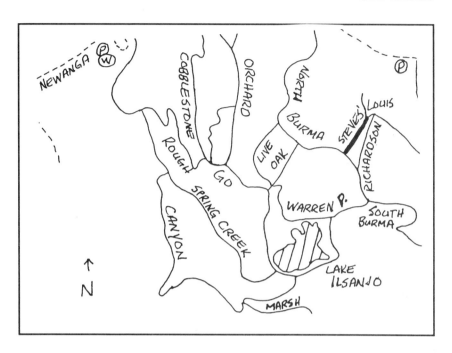

Connector from N. Burma to Louis ❶

The rest of Steve's was regrettably closed in the autumn of 1989. This stretch is just a short connector that is a fairly wide smooth wandering fire road through a pretty clearing - smooth and slightly downhill to Louis.

LOUIS TRAIL
.12 miles

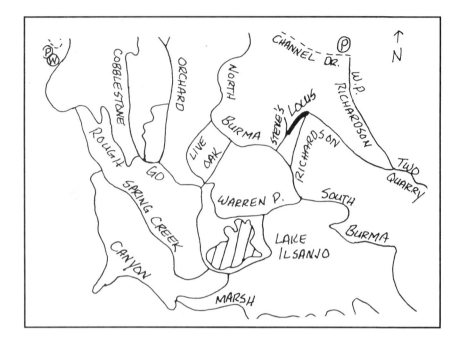

From Steve's S to WPR   ❷

The Louis Trail is a very short but fun trail with a couple of 'stair steps' and large roots to negotiate through a nice grove of new growth redwoods. A large mud hole blocks the middle during the winter - great fun! There is a picnic table at the intersection with Warren P. Richardson that would be a good, shady spot for a break on those hot summer days.

WARREN P. RICHARDSON
3.4 miles

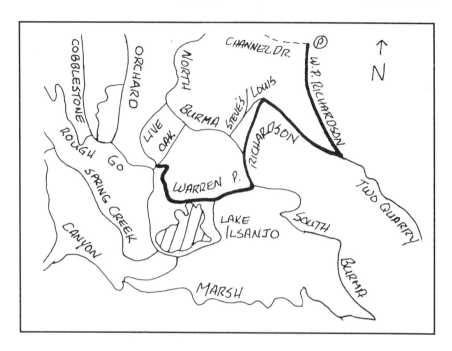

From the park entrance at end of Channel Drive
.78 miles - intersection with Two Quarry ❷
1.5 - picnic stop on side of trail ❸
1.9 - intersection with Louis (a picnic stop in redwood grove) ❸
2.2 - intersection with N. Burma ❶
2.4 - intersection with S. Burma ❶
2.8 - intersection with Middle Steve's ❶
3.4 - end of trail at Live Oak and Rough Go ❶

Warren P. Richardson Trail is the main thoroughfare of Annadel
State Park. Starting at the main parking lot at the end of Channel
Drive, the road begins as a wide, flat, smooth fire road with a slightly
moderate climb. At the intersection with Two Quarry the road turns
sharply to the right and begins to climb fairly steeply. The trail is
frequently covered with a deep layer of gravel which makes traction
'interesting'! Downhill riders should be particularly careful. The
climb is shaded the whole way. The road peaks for the most part at
the intersection with Louis Trail, where there is a good spot for a
picnic amid a stand of new growth redwoods. From Louis out to North

and South Burma the road is wide flat open and smooth - easy pedaling. The road remains a beginners paradise on by Middle Steve's and down by Lake Ilsanjo, where there are more great spots for a break. You can swim in the lake!! Notice the restrooms by the side of the trail. A gentle climb on the continuing wide smooth fire road brings the rider to the end of the trail at its intersection with Live Oak and Rough Go.

SOUTH BURMA TRAIL
1.92 miles

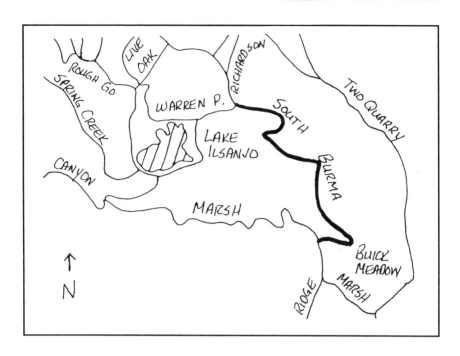

From Warren P. Richardson
1.3 - Basalt Trail to left is now closed to bikes ❸
1.4 - Scenic Overlook ❸
1.92 - intersection with Marsh Trail (end of S. Burma) ❸

South Burma is a trail whose changing conditions provide a good ride for an intermediate rider and will test a beginner. The road climbs from Warren P. Richardson and is the usual Annadel rock garden. This is definitely a ride, requiring a combination of leg strength and skill that may have a beginner walking a bit. There is lots of mud in the winter! The scenic overlook looks west toward the coast and has a picnic table in a manzanita grove - a good rest spot after the climb. This is the quickest route between the easy cruising areas of Lake Ilsanjo and Buick Meadow.

TWO QUARRY
1.98 miles

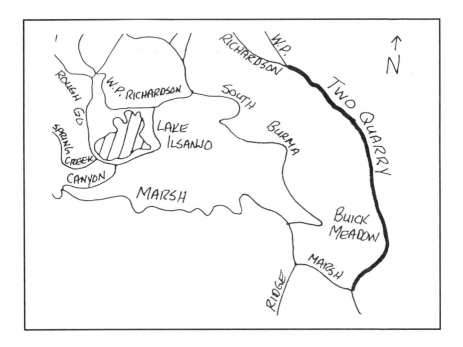

From WPR
.25 miles - trail up to the right is Basalt, which is closed to bikes.
Believe me - you wouldn't want to ride it anyway! ❶
1.36 - park entrance at Frey Canyon Overlook ❶
1.98 - intersection with Marsh Trail (end of Two Quarry) ❷

Two Quarry uphill is a long grinder of a 'fire road' that is actually more like a single track. The road is solid rocks the size of melons that make the passage extremely technical. Determination not to be stopped is the key to 'cleaning' Two Quarry. Just as you hit a spot in the middle to catch your breath, you hit a large unshaded stretch that, in the summer, is particularly brutal. The road climbs steadily with only a moderate grade, but it is the constant rocky surface that demands attention, and saps the will a bit. This might be a better downhill! The top half from Frey Canyon Overlook to Marsh still climbs steadily before descending to the end, but the surface changes considerably to a wide flat smooth fire road - no more rocks! There is lots of horse traffic in the area, so please be aware. There is a picnic table and restrooms at the intersection with Marsh - a good spot for a break after climbing Two Quarry.

MIDDLE STEVE'S S
.3 miles

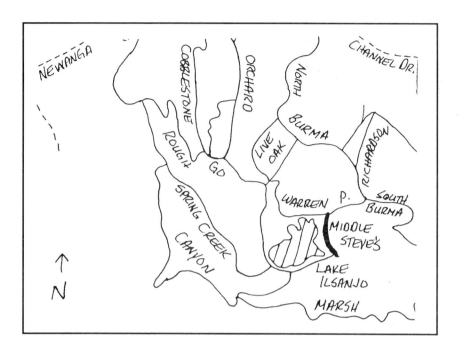

From Warren P. Richardson to Canyon ❶

This short shot is one of two brief sections of Steve's S Trail that remain open to mountain bikes. This fire road runs uphill from Canyon, alongside the shore of Lake Ilsanjo and connects with Warren P. Richardson, completing a ride around the lake. The surface is wide, flat and smooth - easy pedaling for everyone. One of the few restrooms in the park is located here.

MARSH TRAIL
4.20 miles

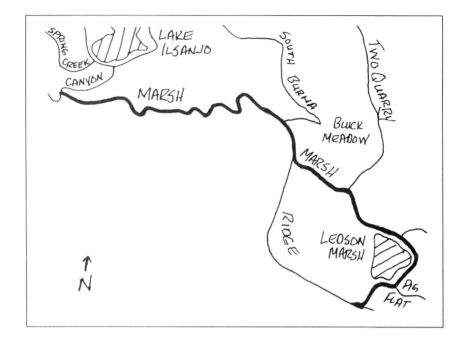

From Canyon at Lake Ilsanjo to the end at Ridge Trail

2.02 - Upper Steve's ❸

2.38 - South Burma at Buick Meadow ❸

2.68 - North End of Ridge Trail ❷

3.08 - Two Quarry ❶

3.38 - Rhyolite Trail (closed to bikes) ❶

3.62 - Lawndale ❶

3.80 - Pig Flat ❶

4.20 - South End of Ridge Trail (end of Marsh) ❷

Marsh is one the the main roads in the park. Starting from Lake Ilsanjo, it climbs steadily with a moderate grade up toward Buick Meadow. There are the ubiquitous Annadel rocks in the trail, making the 'fire road' more of a single track. Coming down, this very bumpy section hammers the arms and shoulders mercilessly - but what fun! There are always lots of horses around, so please ride in control. The trail intersects both Upper and Middle Steve's S trails, which were recently closed to bikes. The climb ends at the intersection of South Burma at Buick Meadow. Here Marsh becomes a level, wide, flat and smooth cruise of a fire road down to Two Quarry, passing the north end of Ridge Trail en route. At Two Quarry there is a restroom and nice picnic spot. This seems to be a popular stop for all park users, so ride with care. From Two Quarry to the top of Lawndale the road continues as a wide, smooth, easy fire road along the shores of Ledson Marsh, from which the trail gets its name. You will pass the top of the Rhyolite Trail, a very rugged single track that was also recently closed to bicycles. From here the Marsh Trail remains an easy pedal, hugging the shore of the marsh, circling around to Pig Flat, another nice picnic spot. The last stretch of Marsh to its end at the Ridge Trail is wide and flat, but frequently has very deep drainage ruts that can easily throw you for a loop - pay attention!

PIG FLAT TRAIL
.5 miles

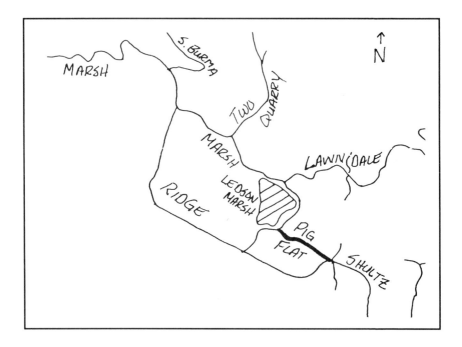

From Pig Flat to Shultz ❷

The Pig Flat Trail is a nice wide easy pedalin' fire road with some small rocks (sound familiar!) that ends in a nice, secluded meadow, at which point it becomes the Shultz Trail.

SHULTZ TRAIL
1.8 miles

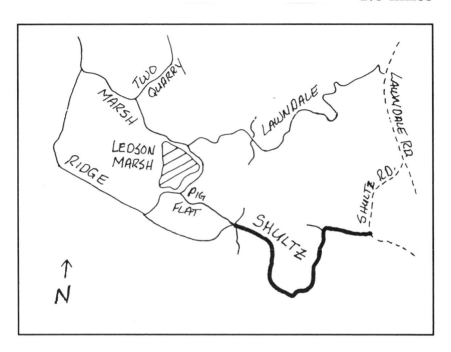

From Pig Flat Trail to end at Shultz Road entrance to Park.
.1 - Power Line access roads to left and right ❶

Shultz Trail is a long, winding downhill that, once again, is more a single track than a fire road due to the extremely rocky, technical conditions that demand constant attention. Hold on and pay attention - this is a great ride! The power line road running to the north is a very short, brush covered road that goes nowhere. The power line road to the south runs downhill for .35 miles and deadends at private property - not much of a ride. Shultz runs in the open near the top, with great views south along the hills. Toward the bottom it becomes mostly shaded, ending at a nearly unknown entry to the park, in a beautifully quiet corner of Sonoma County. The only problem with Shultz presents itself if you want to climb back up to the park. It is a <u>very</u> major grind up either Shultz or Lawndale.

LAWNDALE TRAIL
1.9 miles

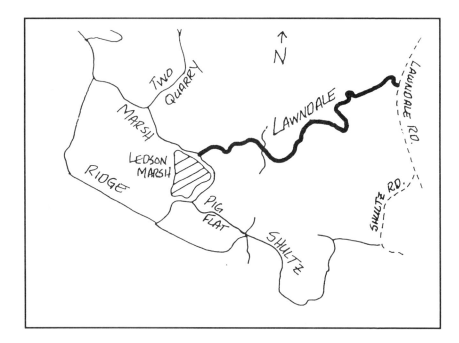

From park entrance at Lawndale Road to Marsh Trail
1.5 - Rhyolite Trail ❶
1.9 - Marsh Trail (the end!) ❸

Lawndale climbs from the parking lot at the south entrance of the Annadel, located on Lawndale Road. The dirt lot has space for perhaps twenty cars, though it is frequently filled with trucks and horse trailers. There are no facilities. The road itself climbs immediately and precipitously. As if the steep grade weren't enough of a test, the surface is very technical; strewn with large rocks and debris from the overhanging trees and always deeply rutted - the Zen of mountain biking. One spot requires choosing between a stretch of muddled rock slabs or channels of loose, rocky 'mush' - good luck! We guarantee that it is makeable. Downhill would, of course, be a bit easier, though not by much. The traction is questionable everywhere. The power line roads near the first 'top' are short and not worth the effort. After these side roads, the trail continues to climb, though not as steeply. There are always those fun rocks in the trail, so you can never get up a good head of steam. At least the first climb is in the shade. Up here, when you have just about had it - you are totally exposed to the hot sun. But now you are up. The rest is almost all easy (the key word here is almost!).

RIDGE TRAIL
2.17 miles

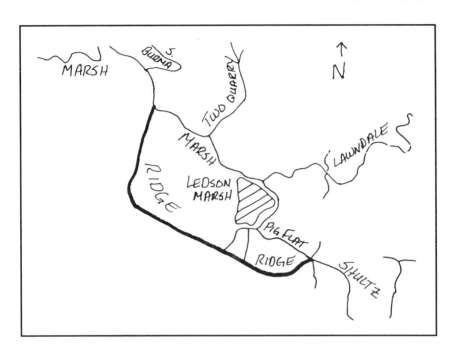

From Shultz to Marsh
.7 - Dan's Trail ❸
.77 - south end of Marsh Trail ❷
1.47 - Steve's S Trail ❸
2.17 - north end of Marsh Trail ❸

The Ridge Trail is an interesting, scenic ride along the west border of the park. From Shultz Trail it starts as a fun, little single track through a secluded meadow that does have its tricky sections - including a tight rut that tends to throw the unwary rider into a large patch of poison oak. At Dan's Trail the road widens and smooths out, becoming an easy cruise. Dan's is a short, easy cut back toward Pig Flat (.2 miles). Now the road climbs and drops along a great old stone fence that separates the park from some very nice private homes. Two significant hills rise through open fields, heading towards Bennett Mountain, the highest point in the park. You will not be climbing to the summit however, as the trail veers off to the right. Steve's S Trail, at the point of this 'veer', is a very steep, unstable hillclimb that is now closed to bikes. The road along here is fairly wide and easy to ride, though as always you need to pay attention. The last stretch is a great long downhill run with the ever present rocks to keep things interesting. Watch out for horses and hikers.

CANYON TRAIL
2.31 miles

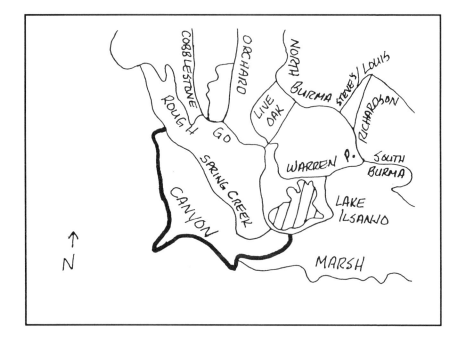

From Middle Steve's at Lake Ilsanjo
.21 - Rough Go ❶
.71 - Marsh Trail ❶
2.31 - Spring Creek Trail ❷

The Canyon Trail is perhaps the easiest way up and down from the plateau that is central Annadel. From the top at Lake Ilsanjo the road is wide, flat and smooth, though peppered with the usual Annadel rocks in spots. At the intersection with Marsh, there is a nice, shaded spot with a picnic table. Down from Marsh the trail descends with a reasonable grade that would be rideable for almost any cyclist in either direction. The bottom third is a level run along the side of the hill, ending at the intersection with Spring Creek. The initial gentle rise and gradually increasing grade do make this the best way for a novice cyclist to make the inevitable climb to Lake Ilsanjo and the rest of the great trails on the top.

SPRING CREEK TRAIL
2.16 miles

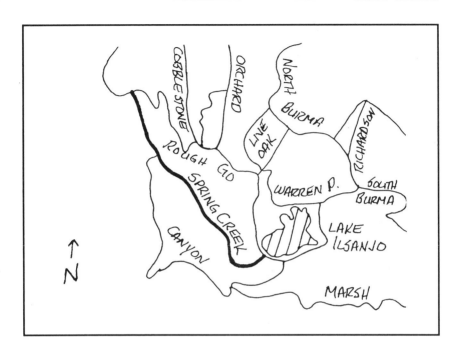

From Lake Ilsanjo to Oak Knolls Picnic Area
1.16 - Canyon Trail ❸
.50 - Rough Go (Annadel Entrance) ❶
.50 - Oak Knoll Picnic Area (Spring Lake Park) ❶

Spring Creek from Lake Ilsanjo drops quickly and is the usual Annadel rocky, bumpy ride - weaving your way in and out of lots of small, sharp rocks. You have to stay on top of things. After the initial descent, the road levels out and becomes a beautiful shaded cruise along the creek, which has at least some water in it year round. There is one deep, tricky gully to cross, so don't let your mind wander too much. From the intersection of Canyon to Rough Go the the trail is wide, smooth and level - easy pedaling. It tends to be heavily gravelled, which makes the ride a bit 'mushy', but shouldn't be a problem. The last stretch from Rough Go to Oak Knoll travels the edge of the park and is a wide, smooth, flat ride along the creek, easy for anyone. Spring Creek would be a good ride up into the park for intermediate riders looking for a good workout to start the day's ride.

ROUGH GO
2.19 miles

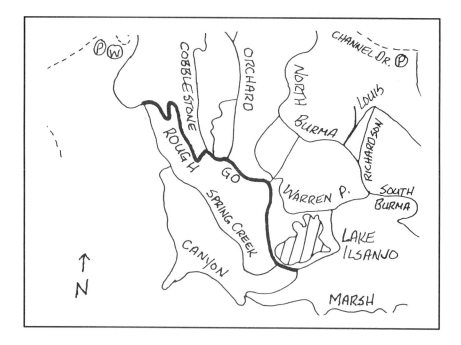

From Canyon to Spring Creek
.25 - quick single track up to Warren P. Richardson ❷
.73 - Live Oak Trail ❷
.77 - Orchard Trail ❷
.78 - a great single track winding over the hill to Orchard at False Lake Meadow - do it!
.80 - Cobblestone Trail ❷

Rough Go is aptly named. It is just that - a very rough, bumpy ride over lots of unforgiving rocks. The top section from Canyon to Cobblestone is actually not so bad - a moderately bumpy, but fairly level run by Lake Ilsanjo and across the southern edge of False Lake Meadow. Look for mud in the winter. From Cobblestone down to Spring Creek, however, you are in for a pounding, as the trail drops sharply. Don't worry about excessive speed. You will be on the brakes heavily as you attempt to pick a path through the rocks. This is not recommended as a route up into the park, but it is makeable. It is also not recommended as a route either way for the entry level cyclist - take Spring Creek or Canyon.

ANNADEL STATE PARK

Annadel State Park is a mountain biking paradise just one hour north of Marin, in the Sonoma County town of Santa Rosa. Over thirty miles of trails and fire roads climb, fall, twist and turn around its 5,000 acres of scenic wilderness.

Annadel was originally inhabited by the Southern Pomo and Southern Wappo Indians, though no permanent village sites have been found in the park. The 18th century arrival of the Spanish changed the area into a cattle ranching and farming center, with the park area being included in a land grant of 19,000 acres in 1837. By the late 1800rds the the area had become an important quarrying site, as the demand for cobblestones in San Francisco grew. A days riding in Annadel will leave you with little doubt about its suitability as a quarry. There are rocks everywhere and most of the routes are reminiscent of cobblestone streets - bumpy, bumpy, bumpy!

The park's name comes from the grand-daughter of the Hutchinson family, who were principal land owners of the area at the turn of the century. Apparently the area was then known as 'Annie's Dell'. The area became a state park in 1971. The land and climate are very similar to Marin, with sweeping open meadows punctuated by thick stands of Douglas fir, bay and redwood. Here also are the rugged, rocky hillsides studded with manzanita. Daytime temperatures can be a bit hotter than Marin in summer and a bit colder in winter. **There is no drinking water at all once you get up into the park! Carry lots of water.**

Lake Ilsanjo, in the middle of the park, was named after Ilsa and Joe Coney, who owned the land from the 1930's until it became a park. You can swim in the Lake! False Lake Meadow, at the northern end of the park, is a beautiful meadow in the summer and fall. In the winter it is no longer 'false'! Ledson Marsh, to the west, is a great place for birding, as numerous species inhabit the reeds throughout the year. Most of the year the park's trails are dry and hard, but winter rains turn Annadel into a giant mudbath - great riding! Just remember to bring clothing that will keep you warm when wet. You can only get so wet! Also remember that, just as in Marin, there is poison oak everywhere. It can get you year round, so learn to identify it and steer clear.

We have always parked in Spring Lake County Park, at the east edge of Annadel. The entrance is on Violetti Rd., off Channel Drive. There is a day use fee of $2. per car. This park has a swimming hole, restrooms and a snack bar and a nice, paved bike path around Spring Lake. Free parking is available at the other end of Channel Drive, but the facilities are minimal. The ranger's office is located along Channel Drive, about halfway between Spring Lake and the free parking lot. Annadel is liberally laced with unnamed trails heading off in all directions. Most of them are short connections between the main trails, particularly around Lake Ilsanjo and in the northeast corner of the park. We have attempted to describe all of ones that are worth riding. **The trails in general are always in a state of change, with seasonal weather patterns and park maintenance. We cannot be held responsible for their condition on any given day. You should always ride with care. We recommend that you contact the park before riding to inquire about current conditions. For information call the Annadel State Park Ranger Station at (707) 539-3911.**

ANNADEL

STATE PARK

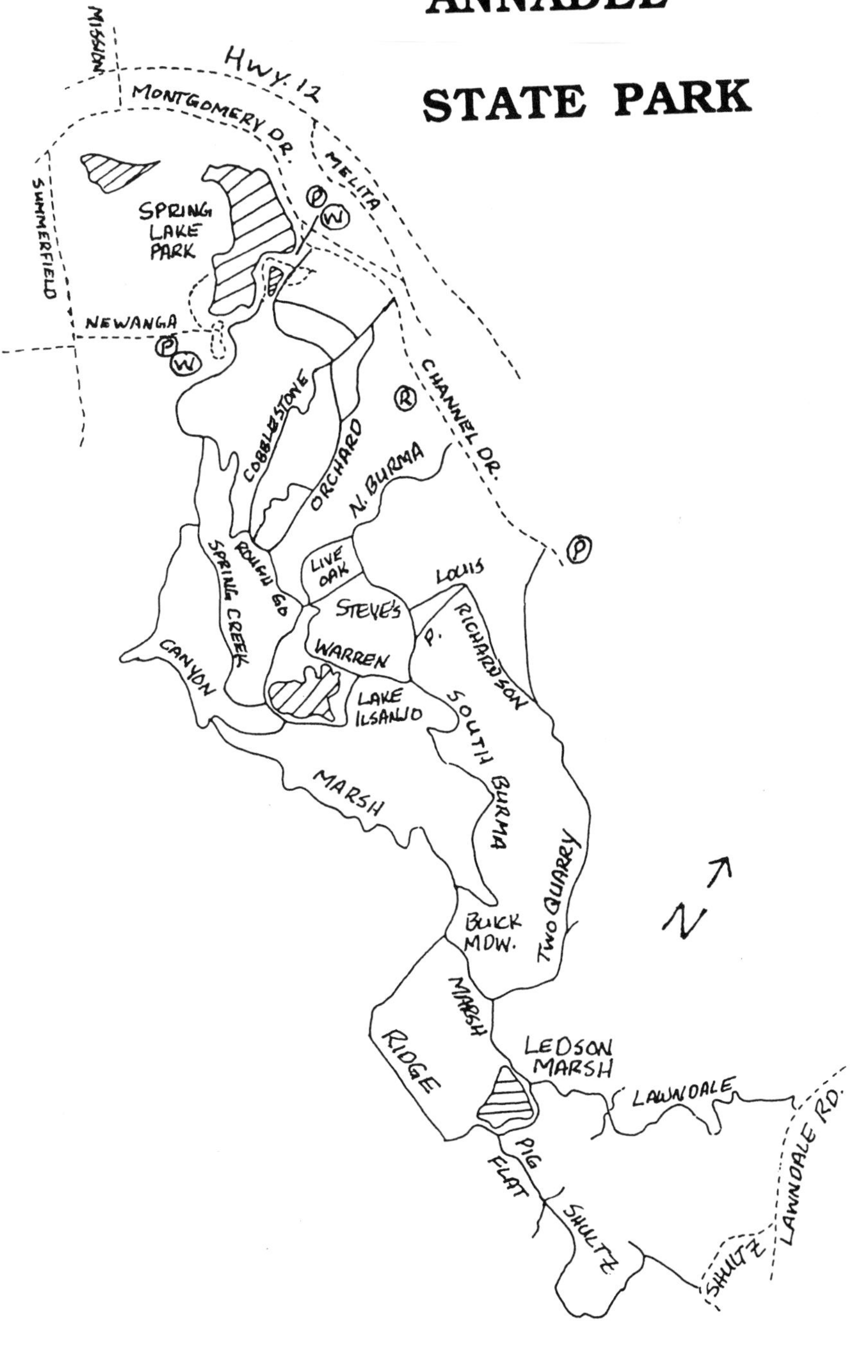

MISSION

Hwy. 12

MONTGOMERY DR.

MELITA

SUMMERFIELD

SPRING LAKE PARK

NEWANGA

CHANNEL DR.

COBBLESTONE

ORCHARD

N. BURMA

ROUGH GO

SPRING CREEK

LIVE OAK

LOUIS

STEVE'S

RICHARDSON

CANYON

WARREN

LAKE ILSANJO

SOUTH BURMA

MARSH

TWO QUARRY

BUICK MDW.

MARSH

LEDSON MARSH

RIDGE

LAWNDALE

LAWNDALE RD.

PIG FLAT

SHULTZ

SHULTZ

N

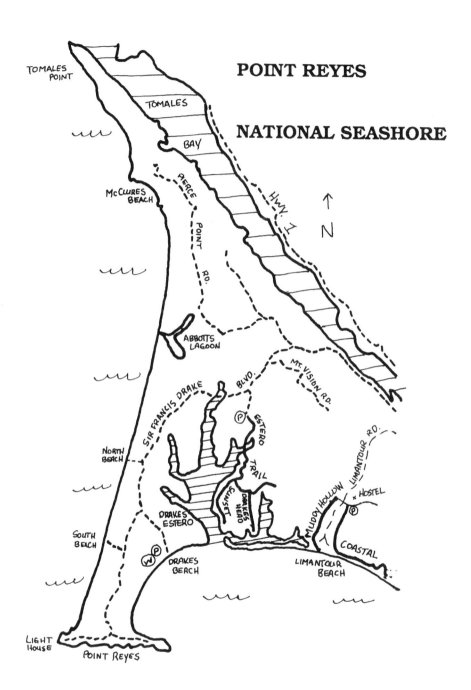

POINT REYES

NATIONAL SEASHORE

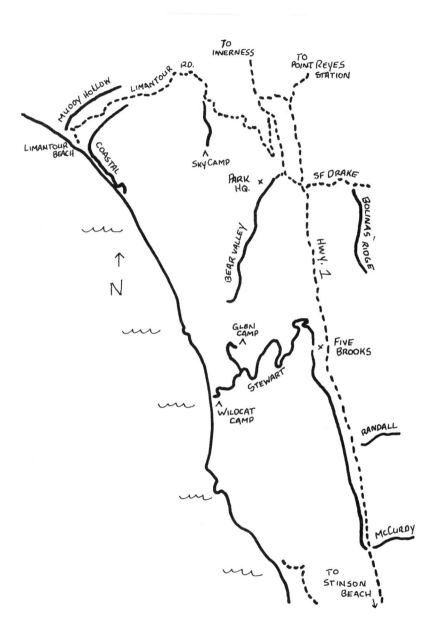